Undressed Relationships Vol. II

Boost
your emotional capital

Dr. Roch

(José Gerardo González Rocha Ph.D.)

Title: Undressed Relationships Vol. II

Subtitle: Boost your emotional capital

ISBN #978-1-955201-12-4

For any requirement, email: admon@directoconsultores.mx

Website: www.drroch.mx

Whatsapp: +52 (477) 799 6718

Find me on any social media platform as "drrochoficial" Facebook, YouTube, Instagram, twiter, spotyfy, tik tok, linkedin, iTunes, audible, kindel, Amazon, barnes and noble.

EmprendeDoer *Publishing*

Teléfono: +1 (916) 308 3540

editorialemprendedores@gmail.com

Second Edition

Printed in the United States of America

About the Author

José Gerardo González Rocha, better known as Dr. Roch is a speaker and writer, he has a PhD in Organizational Behavior and Human Resources Management from Newport University and a Master's Degree in Organizational Development. He's also a certified platinum member of the Global Network of Speakers in Germany.

For over 30 years he's been dedicated to training people and organizations in order to strengthen them according to the requirements they have in their path towards success.

He gives his groundbreaking EBE method (Evidence-Based Execution) in different workshops, seminars, and lectures; activities he does along with his love for magic. He also stands out with his application, evidence, investigations and interpretations of reality with the thymus.

Among his books are: La Magia de Los Negocios que no Quiebran, Reingeniería Personal, Caminos de la Creatividad, and Fábrica de Estrellas.

Presentation

Thank you for assuming the challenge of reading this book. I give you every word with all the respect you deserve as a human being, as well as a blessing for knowing we're related and connected.

A healthy relationship with anyone requires a healthy relationship with yourself and the Voice's Spirit. I am also bewildered with this life that lacks logic and in order to open the door to its secrets, we need to be cultivated and experience pain, to look at ourselves with humbleness...

Although we search for the best, we don't get it easily. Perhaps, when trying to develop a relationship, a project, or a business, you have hurt others and you've been hurt. Maybe you've been betrayed, you've felt alone. Surely, you have experienced frustration and hopelessness.

I know it hasn't been easy and you've fought to be happy. I invite you to give yourself the benefit of the doubt. Dare to try something new, and observe if your reality improves, as mine has. Remember that, on this path, you and I will fail over and over again until we achieve success.

Introduction

These two volumes will help you interpret your reality better, and will teach you how to establish meaningful bonds with yourself, the other people, the universe, and your spiritual dimension, allowing you to make the necessary arrangements so you can be fulfilled, here and now!

Undressed relationships are the result, and at the same time, the reason of a meaningful life. They are in the present and only appear after overcoming one's hopelessness, inferiority complex, defeatism, hate, anger, and guilt. The undressed side refers to the Spirit's transparency and the awareness that we are one with the people surrounding us, the universe, and God.

These two books will attempt to show you the different dimensions of the undressed relationships, so you can get rid of what's superfluous and explore their beauty and kindness, that are often hidden behind several masks; so you can rescue your essence and uniqueness, and recognize the uniqueness of others, and then establish fulfilling relationships.

In this **Volume II of Undressed Relationships,** I'll explain to you everything you need to know to strengthen your relationships, while the second part of *Lourdes' trip* will show you the extraordinary consequences of undressing the spirit when we have to love.

Evidence-Based Execution (EBE)

What I write is based on real evidence of what works and what doesn't work within relationships; it's the results of what I have studied and the experience I've gathered in about thirty years of working with companies, football teams, artists, singers, politicians, families, couples, and emotional and personal learning partners.

In my workshops, I use the Evidence-Based Execution: I don't care if you don't believe what I say, you will gather enough evidence as you apply the ideas I share, which were extracted from my experience and education.

Sometimes, we need specific ideas to improve ourselves. I think of myself twenty years ago, and what I would have wished a practical counselor guiding me would say. The reinforcement and confirmation help you act with confidence.

You may not agree with these ideas. Sometimes, my students rebel against some of them, but it's on them to choose if they want to feel like they are right or if they prefer to follow what works.

It doesn't matter if you hesitate regarding my reflections, the important thing is to challenge the way you live your daily life.

Getting to know the perspective of someone you don't have a close relationship with allows you to avoid being defensive, or triggering your defense mechanism. Perhaps it's easier to read here what your significant other or a friend wants you to see.

Hearing from someone more of what you already know allows you to become confident and change the way you approach reality.

Life is a mystery, but the reality is powerful. It's necessary to find the truth beyond what the **Mind that Lies.** tells us, that voice that keeps repeating you're innocent, that everything you've done has been good, and that fighting is not worth it because life doesn't matter.

I'll be thankful if you shared with me the results you obtained using my recommendations, so more people can implement them in their lives. I'm particularly interested in the real and practical things. If just one person could improve his or her existence through the ideas expressed in here...

Chapter 1

Undressed relationships for couples

An undressed relationship with a life partner is a natural consequence that comes after having established an undressed relationship with yourself.

But TV shows and video clips show something totally different, because love doesn't happen instantly, it is gradually strengthened, and despite being one of the most important aspects in the majority of people's lives, it's one of those things we don't know much about.

You're probably convinced that, in order to be happy, you need to break your heart over and over again. Luckily, that is not true.

"Love doesn't consist of gazing at each other, but looking outward together in the same direction."
Antoine de Saint-Exupéry

We are "everything," and we're formed by our physical, mental, and spiritual existence, and, by the same token, our experience regarding what we call "love" involves these three spheres.

An undressed relationship in a couple seems to be the most complete scenario in which we can explore and experience those three spheres as a whole.

Relationships according to the level of understanding

1. Physical

We spend time together, do activities together, and talk about what happens to us. We need each other's company. It could be said that this is the dimension in which platonic love is developed.

2. Sensual

We enjoy the pleasure of being together, although we don't get involved in other aspects. This is the case of lovers or "friends with benefits."

3. Emotional

We're interested in loving and taking care of each other, we play and behave like children. We tell ourselves a thousand times that we love each other, as if this guarantees an eternal relationship. Relationships developed in this dimension reveal certain insecurities that make both people reaffirm what they feel every single moment.

4. Mental or intellectual

This dimension implies competency regarding our intellect, but this doesn't add any value in the relationship. Doing the best according to the habits, beliefs, and social expectations is what it's looked for. Although there's a lot of theory about love, a relationship based on the intellect gets cold because it's experienced by the MIND THAT LIES.

5. Spiritual

Relationships in this dimension look for sharing the meaning of life, loving beyond ourselves, because there's a mission above us that we share, without missing our north. There's no competition but collaboration and joy, because we have the knowledge we need to overcome the selfish tendency of desiring to be loved.

The real, authentic, and genuine relationships are the ones displayed in this dimension, nevertheless, they aren't something static, but an evolving process that's relying on small and amorous behaviors which are done with humbleness every day.

Learn to identify your relationships

Undressed relationships belong to the spiritual dimension and they happen in couples, as well as with friends, people that share faith or a vision for life, teachers and students, family...

All of the relationships are potentially dynamic, that is to say, they come and go through different dimensions, they can be clearly defined, or we can perceive their limits as blurred.

Sometimes, one phase is joined to the other one and the person goes over them, like climbing stairs. In other cases, people are stuck in one dimension and they don't move forward, which generates a huge risk.

It's important to not judge or make permanent decisions based on our mood or when a relationship is going through a hard time.

As far as we learn to read the reality the Spirit proposes, life will show us with clarity the path, and the willingness to follow it will become a habit that will make us better, because that's the whole purpose of relationships in our life: allowing us to learn the lessons we need in order to evolve.

The physical and sensual dimensions run out quickly, due to their superficial nature, forcing us to move to another love.

On the other hand, it's very common to stay stuck in the mental or intellectual dimensions, where the **MIND THAT LIES** distracts us with its tricks, making us avoid the spiritual dimension, where we'll actually find fulfillment in our relationship.

Thinking "I want to beloved" makes us avoid an undressed relationship.

As you'll see, the desired undressed relationship regarding couples is a treasure we would only find after overcoming certain obstacles within ourselves.

Mirages in an undressed relationship

E specially regarding romantic love, there are some situations we want to avoid if we want to achieve authentic bonds. I'll give you a list of the most important aspects you must consider if you want to achieve an undressed relationship below.

Falling in love with "love"

People are very focused on their minds, they easily fall in a "game" of love which consists of loving the state of love. They get absorbed by interchanging abstractions and if they find coincidences, they feel attracted, although, at heart, they're attached to ideas like clothes on a rack.

The problem is that when reality knocks on the door, they find there was no foundations in their relationship. They have to recognize that, instead of loving, they had been avoiding reality, like someone trying to escape from prison, but in these cases, instead of leaving prison, they get in.

These couples tend to stay away from other people, getting encased in what they consider "a love that's out of this world." The problem is that this isn't love, although it is actually out of this world.

Sooner or later, time or any event will make the unrealistic bubble explode, waking them up from that vision. They'll find out they were in the mind's dungeon, built with illusions, away from reality.

Possessive "love"

Possessive love is just a way to make the "loved" person an object. In these cases, phrases like "you're mine" or "you're for me" tend to be very natural, nevertheless, those phrases need to be analyzed.

When you accept being an object, you lose your identity and dignity.

When losing yourself, you stop being your lover's partner, and he or she will end up looking for someone else that fills the spot you left empty, because you became his or her object instead.

The consequences mental love produces are catastrophic. Normally, it happens when people get filled with expectations that reality can't satisfy. Frustration becomes so big, that they decide to withdraw their intellectual love, leaving their partners heartbroken for not having achieved their requirements.

Mental love generates disappointment, sadness, anxiety, powerlessness, loss, and frustration.

But, these items also matter, because, as human beings, nothing makes us more perfect than our imperfections, because they mean we can always try to achieve a higher level of fulfillment.

Changing our vision for a more realistic approach
and getting rid of expectations
heal the wounds we got from this type of love.

Jealousy

Hand in hand with possessive mental love, there's jealousy. This vortex makes you want the other one to be "yours" and "only for yourself," as though he or she was your favorite toy. This type of attitude is linked to insecurity and lack of self-esteem.

Jealous people don't feel they have the necessary traits to make the person they love stay with them and those who tolerate that attitude have such a low self-esteem that consider what they're being subjected to as a demonstration of love, when it's actually the opposite.

Jealousy can improve the flavor of relationships like vanilla can improve a cake if you use just a little bit, but using too much can destroy even the most exquisite relationship—and cake.

Dependency and codependency

One of the hardest mirages to overcome in order to achieve authentic relationships is caused by dependency and codependency. When there's dependency, one of the two needs the other and tends to act as someone inferior. I've met "couples" that actually look like a boss and an employee, father and daughter, or mother and son. Dependent people haven't learned how to be autonomous and this stops them from forming healthy relationships.

Many books have been written about codependency, because it's a common problem in relationships and, plenty of times, relationships tend to fail because of it.

When there's codependency, generally there's a deficiency, a vice, a problem, or an illness, whether real or imaginary, in one of the two, and that makes the other one act as a savior. As a consequence, both become addicted to their role and they can't be anything else when they're together.

It's very common to find codependency in alcoholic families, compulsive players, drug addicts. This type of mirage not only shows up in lovers, it also shows up in parents and children.

*An ideal undressed relationship
would be interdependent.*

Nevertheless, this is only possible when both transcend their idealizations and fantasies, focusing on their personal development and on a common mission in life, beyond themselves.

Love and freedom are like two sides of the same coin. There's no way one can exist without the other. Someone who's actually able to love respects the other one's space and someone free loves with honesty, without masks or tricks.

Nevertheless, it might seem that freedom in love disappears after a commitment, especially in long-term relationships, however, this idea follows a wrong interpretation of life.

Nowadays, no one gets in a relationship against their will. If we promised to be in one, our freedom must be loyal to it.

In the Judeo-Christian tradition, God tends to promise, therefore, promises don't destroy freedom, because the Supreme Being is the absolute freedom.

If we were created in His image and likeness, we are also able to experience our promises with freedom.

When routine destroys passion

Passion for something gives us energy, making us a sort of vitabites warehouse for whenever we need them. Don't let low energy undermine your life and relationships, put some passion in them!

A vitabyte is the unit of the vital energy we feel and project when we feel good and live according to what we are. This is the result of a coherent life and the capacity to correct ourselves when needed.

Passion is something you can't fake. It's that inner strength that pops up when you have a purpose connected to your inner being that boosts you to achieve it. Passion is a decision, but it's also a connection. It's achieved when what you do externally is aligned with your inner purpose. If your only ambition is to have an easy life without problems, you're mistaken; life doesn't work that way.

People who haven't found passion live sad and poor lives. A life without challenges is a life without passion and, now more than ever, passionate people are needed by the whole world, people able to transform their reality and, mostly, people willing to maintain the same state of commitment for a long-term basis.

Passion is shown with facts. There are people with really good intentions, but in their daily lives they forget they responsibilities or just do them unwillingly, making mistakes, because they lack passion and are bored of the routine.

Passion is the salt of life. Season your life!

Living without passion is living halfway. A passionate couple is the one that's willing to fall in love every day as they did the first day.

This couple doesn't follow imposed stereotypes nor follow "the right thing." but expresses feelings in creative and stimulating ways and it's willing to get back on track whenever the waves make it go in another direction. Try to give to your experiences something to vitalize them.

Pretending to be someone you're not

It's not right to become an awful person during the relationship and then blame your partner. It's not also loyal becoming a better person and feeling superior and, then, abandoning your partner.

Each one of you should assume the responsibility of improving yourselves in the relationship, the other person didn't cause what we became, for better or for worse. They're not a hero nor a villain.

In one of my workshops of Undressed Relationships, one of the participants asked a powerful question, "Dr. Roch, how do you recognize a valuable relationship? How do you know it's not about a layer of ego or imagination, or a projection of our ideas onto the person we decide to love, or just a simple disguised sexual instinct? How to distinguish between schizophrenia and a miracle?"

This type of question can confirm how fascinating and complex "love" is. That simple term that actually hides several layers.

Love is lived, experienced. It's not a simple intellectual concept nor a mental process, because it's action. It's a real experience, it's about commitment, it's an experience that improves your reality and your partner's reality, because he or she goes with you in this path in order to achieve mutual growth.

This is a contemplation of what we are, in essence, without any sort of shame. Pure manifestation coming out of the limits of the self. It's the capacity to understand that we are way more than what we can express, write, talk, feel, and even experience... We are infinite!

Undressed relationships go beyond temporary limits, expanding until breaking expectations, stereotypes, and limitations.

Being "happy"

Before you can be happy with someone, you need to live your existence as a unique human being, truthful to what you are. Happiness is not what life and reality give you from outside, but what you do with what you are given.

It's not a goal, it's not something you can ask of someone else. If you want to get it, you need to do it for yourself, there's no other way.

When I do what my reality asks of me, happiness goes along with me and I thank it for that. But it's not something I can hold or possess. That state is the result of what you're being when living peacefully in your reality.

Happiness is appreciating who you are
while trying to get to your goal.

When you're happy and find another person that's also happy, the relationship can only improve that happiness. Finding the right person who is happy and someone worth starting a relationship with, is one of the main desires I hear in my workshops about Undressed Relationships.

"How do I attract someone valuable to my life? How can I find someone worth the risk?" The key is in nature itself. If you observe properly, you'll notice a pig going out with a sow, a duck with a duck... When searching for a relationship, you'll find someone like you.

People that enjoy criticism get along with other people that enjoy it.

Bitter people go out to have a coffee and complain about everything and everyone. In a company, mediocre people gather with mediocre people and criticize the boss that encourages them to be efficient.

We attract people like us. They say we are the average of the five people we spend the most time with, because "if you lie down with wolves, you learn how to howl."

Remember that if we're life energy, we work like a magnet that attracts or rejects. When vibrating, we resonate in people like us, so finding a significant other based on mental classifications and a list of traits doesn't make any sense. It's more effective to be focused on cultivating a good relationship with yourself, getting to know yourself, understanding who you are, what you want, what you're looking for, so you can resonate with the person who's going to be good for you.

The type of person you find in your way
will depend on the quality of your soul.

Idealizing one's significant other

A healthy and real relationship should be established with someone real and balanced. However, no matter how obvious it may seem, this basic requisite isn't always fulfilled.

Some people marry their illusions, the ghost of their father, their favorite movie character, or the star of their dreams.

Relationships are bidirectional, like a two-way street that requires balance, so traffic and empty lanes should be avoided.

Relationships are like streets
that connect you from one place to another.

First, they may look like simple alleys, they might become dirty roads, but then they'll be two-way paved streets and, while you're using them, highways or bridges may appear. A strong and solid relationship is based on this.

Are the opposites... attracted?

In order to move on with your life, you'll have to get a warrior filled with wounds and scars that goes with you, helping you overcome obstacles in this reality; no one is prepared to avoid the surprises that life gives us.

Life stirs all of us up at some point. The question is, how do we move on from the hardships that hurt us? How do I cure my wounds so I don't feel hurt every time I am touched?

Looking for our "soulmate"

We have this wrong idea that, in order to be happy, we need a partner. Relationships aren't supposed to make us happy, but to heal us and make us aware, to help us evolve and improve as people.

Your relationships manifest the relationship you have with yourself. The goal of any relationship is to make those involved into better versions of themselves. We reflect upon the other people what we are and see within us.

Life heals us through our partners.

If your focus is to make your partner happy, that attitude becomes something of an emotional aggression. People that make that mistake get surprised when being abandoned. "But I just tried to make him happy," or "I gave him everything!"

How can one explain that that was the reason his or her loved one ran away scared?

I know this reflection seems to lack logic, mostly if you analyze it based on your dependency—nevertheless, among spiritually healed people, being able to stay reasonably detached is appreciated, because both members of the relationship have enough emotional oxygen. Otherwise, they'll end up getting asphyxiated.

For Erich Fromm, the concept of detachment or the state of being separated is the awareness of our individuality, the perception of being something different than what surrounds us.

Emptiness and frustration

No one can fill the spiritual emptiness of someone else. If you don't heal those things in the relationship with yourself, don't expect someone else to do it for you, because that's unfair and an unreal expectation.

Don't get frustrated if you haven't achieved total fulfillment in this life, that's something that can't be achieved in this temporary life, and it's one of the characteristics of our human nature.

Extraordinary couples have been separated because the man wanted to fill his woman's emptiness, or the woman wanted the man to do so, and this made them feel frustrated, unloved, unheard, neglected.

In a relationship, each person must be able to take ownership of their own wounds and still enjoy the other one's company.

The real purpose of relationships

We don't start a relationship to achieve success, but to grow and design a better reality. If you grow in your relationship, you're ready to have more enriching experiences.

When you're stuck in your relationship, it'll be noticeable in your vitabytes. There are marriages where the spouses basically don't have a common life, whereas some marriages end in pathetic divorces after the two have lived an intense relationship.

I have spent plenty of years investigating this and seeing it for myself, and I've noticed that it's not about focusing on having a long relationship, it's about growing up within it and maintain it alive through mutual attention.

*Relationships are important, mysterious,
and vital in the lives of human beings.*

When routine, different interests, different goals, or taking care of a child grabs the steering wheel, there won't be enough space to park a safe relationship. Working on your relationship requires risk, sacrifice, trust, faith, dedication, but mostly, self-awareness; that is to say, working on your inner side, which is something you can't postpone. It is your relationship's foundation.

The thing with children requires a special analysis. It's ironic, but most couples claim they have perceived a transformation in their relationships the moment they became parents.

A father's love or a mother's love for their children will never change, but this doesn't happen in couples between spouses, and, sometimes, children come to divide that fragile bond. Therefore, it requires to be taken care of, consciously. No one talks about having an ex-son or an ex-father, but it's very frequent to hear people talking about ex-husbands.

There are no happy couples, but happy people in a couple. There aren't also perfect people or couples, although being single isn't great either.

Whatever your sentimental status is, the important thing is to establish undressed relationships, whether they are friendships, marriages, any kinds of bonds, and it's also important to go beyond what you've already achieved.

Authentic relationships can't be sustained in theoretical expectations that come from an absurd perfectionism, and even less from an idealization of love that never comes. The price we pay for those ideas out of this reality is blaming the other person for what our mind created—something that in can't even exist in movies.

*An undressed relationship is one
that's not dominated by the ego.*

Relationships: a delicacy of life

An undressed relationship is a firm relationship that requires strong people able to face the natural adversities in reality without making much drama nor playing the role of the victim or the cominator.

A real undressed relationship
means being able to observe ourselves
and get to know ourselves, seeing the other people
beyond our masks, fears, defenses, and attacks.

Relating with other people is one of the most exquisite experiences in this existence. It's a connection with everything and everyone, our biggest purpose, the huge lesson we came to reveal to each one of us in every encounter, small or big.

Every relationship has the power to make us
approach our divine essence
or our inner destruction.

It's fundamental to know we can always relate to one another, although sometimes it's healthier to physically stay away so we can preserve our inner peace.

When you're in love, your chemistry, thoughts, idealizations, and projections transform you into the least judgmental human being ever. If you make decisions in that mood and then much time passes before you open your eyes, you'll create illusory and unrealistic expectations.

Then you will complain, you will feel frustrated, deceivedand you will be! But it's *your* fault. You ask the other person to change, when the fact is that it's you that must change your expectations.

The ingredients for a healthy and long relationship can be a mystery for many people because they aren't theoretical concepts, recipes, or rules.

The relationship between you
and your significant other is a living process.

Every relationship requires the same things that any human being needs: food, attention, dedication, energy, knowledge, fun, joy, humor, maturity, time. If you don't inject vitabytes into the relationship, it won't blossom. The energy that makes a relationship work can't be changed by something intellectual or theoretical.

I don't know your personal story, but I can suspect that, like most of the people living in this era, the pain and disappointment caused by relationships that ended won't be something strange for you.

Perhaps you've desired to fall in love, to be engaged, or even to get married, but it seems you can't find the right person to do that brave thing. Sometimes, when you think you've found the right person, that relationship doesn't last, your love isn't reciprocated, or the person doesn't wish to commit.

Perhaps you're separated and you're stuck in a river filled with emotional and financial angst, a situation that gets worse if there's conflict regarding taking care of children.

Perhaps your life has been a series
of temporary encounters
that weren't correct for you after all.

In these cases, the result is that you'll be searching for it, filled with a deep, disappointing sensation. If you're a widower, perhaps you aren't w lling to look for a new relationship, or you feel you aren't ready. That safety will come when you understand what you need to give yourself.

If you are in a relationship right now, perhaps you're asking yourself if it will last or if it's "the right person," while you're noticing that your partner isn't like how you believed he or she was.

Perhaps you are still growing up and your partner is stuck, or you don't have the same interests nor support each other in the same way you used to. It's convenient to analyze how you reached that point.

Being single

I know single people with plenty of qualities and a big heart that simply haven't established the correct relationship.

Why didn't I say "they haven't found the right person"? Because I believe we give too much importance to the uncertain and imprecise idea of finding the ideal person in order to have a relationship.

Instead, I bet on building a relationship, that is to say, an action that will have become a daily habit with future results.

In the first half of the past century, it was still common in many countries for parents to choose the lovers of their children. However, there weren't many divorces back then.

Without a doubt, plenty of things weren't beautiful. Back then, women weren't financially independent and breaking up was socially unacceptable.

Nevertheless, not everyone lingered together, resigned. There were also successful marriages where the spouses did everything they could so the relationship could last.

Being single can be a calling and a path of surrendering to art, science, a service career that requires dedication, but it's also an opportunity to build a healthy, honest, unmasked, relationship without defense mechanisms.

We need to understand that a relationship won't make us happy. On the contrary, we need to be happy with ourselves and, in that way, the relationships we get to establish will be well-grounded.

If you haven't found the way of and the pleasure in being alone with yourself, what makes you think it'll be different doing it with someone else?

Everything starts with you.
You are the measurement of your universe.

If you don't know yourself, you'll only be attracting your possible partners to something like an ambush, because what we can offer will depend on what we are.

Our society has demonized being single, but being single is actually a very important moment, because it means there's enough integrity, so you're not looking forward to getting involved with someone to satisfy affective or emotional shortages. Being single allows us to decide who we want in our life when it comes to relationships.

There's a lot of banality and confusion around relationships and their situations, and being single is considered as a **non-relationship**, a shameful situation, or the consequence of being someone who doesn't deserve love which is a big mistake.

The opposite of a healthy relationship with yourself is what's known as emotional codependency. It happens when we form relationships without any special purpose. We just don't want to go through the long periods of solitude that actually come to our life to remind us who we are, what we want, and what we don't want in a relationship.

Many people get into relationships waiting for the other person to take control of their lives. When someone hasn't had the time nor the courage to spend time with themselves and discover themselves, it's likely they will generate unreal expectations when it comes to having a couple, and they'll be disappointed, constantly looking for something that only exists within themselves.

Being single is a privileged stage where you can still remain focused on yourself.

Life in a couple implies a mutual understanding of each other, so being single allows you to get into everything that drives you to become a better version of yourself.

Regarding relationships, being with yourself could be compared to spending a night under the moon. There's no golden splendor from the sunrise, but its silver light also has a charming mystery. You can refuse to accept it and close your eyes until the sun rises or you can recognize its magic and walk under the dark sky.

Just like a caterpillar requires time to become a beautiful butterfly, assume you right to enjoy being single until you decide to change it. Humans are diverse and have different rhythms when it comes to maturing.

Only you decide when's the ideal moment to get into a relationship.

Luckily, younger generations seem to have understood this concept pretty well and they are more and more firm when it comes to being single. That makes me trust in the fact we can have more stable relationships and better marriages in the future.

I've verified in my job as a therapist that it's a mistake to stop being single when we still hold onto past wounds we haven't been able to heal. Being in charge of organizing our feelings and emotions is the same as preparing the field for the seeds. Even if the seed is excellent, it won't grow if it hasn't been prepared

People that have been spiritually healed, establishing undressed relationships are needed in order to overcome today's difficulties. Respecting our moments of loneliness allows us to maintain the necessary balance to generate a difference at every level.

When love tastes like eternity

The real satisfaction in a relationship doesn't come from everything coming out well, but the clear awareness of having chosen that path with freedom, knowing you're being yourself while walking in it, and also letting your significant other be himself or herself.

Marriage is the full collaboration in your life project and your partner's one. An experience about eternity that provides real and constant happiness.

External things can't affect this satisfaction, because our inner side interprets them as a deep state of peace which allows it to make them meaningful and live them as growth experiences, like a spiral, constantly expanding while time passes by.

It's a fulfilled mood that helps you improve your reality, as well as everything surrounding you, because you are complete and whole.

The decision to be together without pretending
to change is the biggest proof of love
that can ever exist between two people.

A marriage based on an undressed relationship is like a rose path that, beside smells and flowers, also has thorns. A relationship is an equation in which the result is way more important than every part of it. This means that it's necessary to assume the commitment, knowing it's going to be necessary to get rid of individual parts if we want to be able to blend with the other person, without losing ourselves entirely.

It seems like a paradox, and perhaps it is. Relationships are considered a sort of intensive course for growth and spiritual evolution. Probably, one of the hardest aspects to assimilate is that, just like human beings go through different stages, the relationships we're in do so too.

One of the things I hear the most from my married patients is that they miss the times before the marriage, that biochemical stage where everything looked like a fairytale, without commitments, but with plenty of illusions. We need to understand that assuming the union called "marriage" implies going to a next level.

Every healthy relationship will need
to become a commitment.

That's the point where most of the conflicts pop up, because people seem to suddenly wake up in a different reality, though this new reality may be something even more real than any other thing they had lived before.

It could be said that while dating is based on our similarities, marriage is based on our differences that precisely restructure us if we know how to make it an alliance and not a war.

Loyalty is the firm decision
of mutual acceptance and remaining together,
no matter what happens.

People fear that living together may kill their passion. I think it can be the opposite, as long as rights and duties are assumed in an undressed way. Our society needs to get back the magic of what I call **the real reality**, not the one we are given through fiction, but the one that exists behind the several masks we use every day in order to hide our human, imperfect, fragile, and fleeting condition.

When our relationships are authentic, real, and undressed, they're also subjected to the same instability, and it's something totally normal, it's normal in any human phenomenon. Every day, it's necessary to check the implicit factors in the relationship, so the necessary adjustments will be made on time, before there's no solution whatsoever.

It's healthy to be aware that love within marriage is amplified and has other shapes, beyond passion, allowing solidarity, empathy, communication, mutual understanding, time, tenderness, and transparency to show up. That's the moment when both of you grow up together.

Living together with commitment is like being in charge of your own garden. You'll need to give it time, you'll have to take care of it every day, so it can flourish like you dream it. Achievements require routine and discipline.

We have this unreal idea telling us we can live a whole life on a cloud of passion, with no attachments, commitments, or structures, but this only reveals that we refuse to grow up as healthy adults.

The **real reality** teaches us that undressed relationships imply assuming the weight of routine as an additional ingredient when being together.

Needing constant novelty isn't but an illusion that most of the time confuses us, leading us to abandon what's important in order to carry what's apparently urgent.

Divorce

We aren't prepared for these days and we haven't investigated deeply how to make families and marriages work.

Back in 1950, after the Second World War, divorce wasn't an easy decision and it was essentially considered an immoral decision. Due to the big censorship that it had, plenty of unhappy married couples remained together, and romantic love disappeared in marriages.

People loved their lovers, while suffering their relationships with their spouses.

They only preserved their marriage to show it in front of society, or because of the children they had.

Years later, divorced became an allowed exit from a broken marriage and while divorce used to be allowed only for instances of mistreatment or infidelity, "incompatibility" ended up becoming an acceptable reason.

Marriage counseling didn't contribute enough to stop divorces, because most of the therapists were fundamentally mediators, helping the couple solve their problems regarding relatives, sex, money, infidelity, loyalty, and children's education, which is something they made based on a contract.

The divorces produced serious problems, because the structure of the family structure started to break under the crushing reality of the failed marriages. Second and third marriages failed even more often, because they were just misguided answers before a marital crisis.

Nowadays, single-parent families, as well as mixed families are considered the rule. All of it is just an adaptation to the problem, an attempt to regulate the cultural realities that have showed up due to our lack of understanding about marriage.

We accept the idea that people shouldn't stay in unhappy marriages and, when these problems show up, we immediately choose to change our partner, when our first choice should be to change the way we live with that person.

*Instead of getting rid of our partner
and maintaining the problem, we should get rid
of the problem and maintain our partner.*

While trying to facilitate things and being more tolerant, we've lost our own needs and real wishes.

We feel disappointed and skeptical before the possibility of a happy marriage, but, as long as we don't recognize the unconscious agenda that interferes when choosing a partner for marriage, families will continue getting fractured, and all of the social problems coming from it will continue affecting us.

On the other hand, if we recognize the necessity of reeducation when it comes to relationships, marriages will survive and thrive and children within marriages will be healthier emotionally.

*I don't care about how elegant
or arranged a divorce is,
experience has shown me
that that isn't the solution nor the answer.*

Children from divorced parents have long-lasting wounds, because, unfortunately, they feel guilty because of their parents' breakup.

Divorce may allow people to escape from a bad marriage, but the effort should be focused on guaranteeing good marriages that boost happiness and individual fulfillment. Otherwise, there will only be detached marriages, problematic children, and a dysfunctional society rising every decade.

Different strategies, different results

We have all sorts of possibilities to establish powerful and life-changing marriages that will revitalize our society. Marriage has a particular potential to facilitate our spiritual growth and heal our wounds, if we are in charge of all of them individually.

We have the wrong idea that one must abandon a marriage in order to grow up and change, but we're finding out that even when there are hardships, it's possible to get a powerful healing if we're in an undressed relationship.

It's not just a rigid institution, marriage is a structure that contains a dynamic process. If it's understood appropriately, an undressed relationship is the therapy we need to grow, be complete, and return to a fulfilling and inner-focused mood.

We need to learn to rectify our relationships, focusing on them as undressed, authentic, and committed bonds, based on experiences, not through perfectionist ideas.

The alternative of being single is an excellent training field for undressed relationships, but it's not a substitute.

Only in the undressed relationship you'll find the necessary ingredients to achieve fulfilling growth and cure yourself. Our attention, concentration, safety, time, the deepest intimacy, and the whole show ourselves reflected through another person.

Only when you commit to accepting your wounds, you'll give your partner a safe space to heal his or her own wounds, to experience their fulfillment, and to capture their original dignity.

We can't heal ourselves, and even less another person, if we don't live in an undressed relationship that allows us to stop lying to ourselves.

Creativity is the essential instrument we need in order to overcome our limits. We need to get educated and trained for the trip that an undressed relationship provides, because it'll make us face everything we don't want to see within ourselves.

Although past relationships remind you of physical pain or failure, they constitute a valuable lesson about things you need to face if you wish to choose and act correctly in the future.

Every past relationship started with attraction and hope. If we dare to observe the past with honesty, recognizing what went wrong, what our unfulfilled expectations were and what our partner's nature was, we'll get an ideal opportunity to see who we are, why we choose what we choose, how we do it, and how we function within relationships.

Recognizing these patterns will help us understand where change and growth is necessary, as well as the nature of the wound that needs to be healed. This way, we'll be prepared for new relationships. When a couple is in the middle of a conflict, it'll be hard for them to be objective. Their memories are confusing and they have their current problems that affect them, sinking deep inside anger and bitterness.

When it comes to past relationships, there's certain level of emotional distance. In these cases, it's easier to evaluate and compare the accumulated data from multiple relationships, as well as to consider your own situation in a long-term period.

Competing or collaborating

I want to share two stories about your conception. In the first one, one of your father's spermatozoa competed with many others, fighting to be the first one. The winner made an incredible and individual effort to reach your mother's still and fertile egg, which waited for it with open doors.

In the second one, which is considered the most recent and realistic one, a man and a woman love each other, and they express their love with intimacy.

After kisses, touching, and stimulating words, the male prepares to shoot a big quantity of spermatozoa inside his partner. The majority aren't fertile, but they are trained to clean the path for those that are fertile. While evading obstacles, the ones that aren't fertile correct the path the best they can, because the goal constitutes a collective task.

After many obstacles, twenty spermatozoa get to their destiny and they get prepared to get in the egg which guides them to the entrance as though it was a magnet.

When all of them are ready, they evaluate themselves to choose the strongest one and one is told, "You're the best of us, please get in and impregnate the egg." This way, although just one of the gets in, all of them will have accomplished the mission.

Perhaps you don't remember this, but when you learned the mission you had, you felt joy and surprise, but you also experienced fear because of the big challenge you had before you.

In order to impregnate the egg, you had to leave your tail that drove you with speed and expertise to the point where you were chosen. When getting in the egg, you were mixed with your mother's biological material and then your story began.

You were chosen, because life is strong
and requires the strongest one to overcome
the challenges that it contains.

All of the stories about fighting to stand out come from the first version of the beginning of life, stepping on the people that interfere.

This type of story makes us feel like warriors, as though we're in a competition, where the only active is the male and the rest of the candidates feel the frustration of almost getting to the goal, but not quite, after the race to impregnate the passive female.

On the other hand, the second version gives us more conciliatory notions. Your life's creative and sexual origin is a huge collaboration between your parents, with a work team of millions of spermatozoa and a huge attraction executed by the egg to help the chosen one to impregnate it.

That was you! The person that's currently reading this book, you turned out to be the strongest and the best one, that's why it doesn't make any sense to think you're mediocre. You were a winner since the beginning.

Your life is a huge miracle made
through collaboration, mutual support,
and common good seeking.

We all have skeletons in our closet, the problem is carrying them everywhere and not letting them go.

Your skeletons are the memories of failures and mistakes you regret and, sometimes, you need to let them go to give yourself the opportunity to start again and initiate new life projects.

Holding on to the past, the fantasy, and a negative version of ourselves makes us commit the same mistakes over and over again. Let yourself be attracted to your dreams like a magnet and merge with them, leaving aside everything that brought you there that you don't need anymore.

Goals aren't achieved in loneliness.

If you've seen scientists, artists, athletes receiving awards, you noticed that the first thing they do is to thank other people, people that helped them achieved their goals.

People who know how to be thankful with the ones that cleaned the path for them have in their hands the power to multiply those results.

You have a wonderful story and it's up to you to take it to a next level, because that's what you were created for.

You were born by that collaborative sexuality.

Become a human being that honors their origin, cultivating a healthy relationship with your sexuality, a collaborative relationship with the other people, transcending the competitiveness and envy, which are the things responsible for your projects' infertility.

Forbidden love

This subject has inspired plenty of wonderful stories in cinema, literature, and the other arts. Romeo and Juliet gave their lives up for a forbidden love.

It was unthinkable that the inheritors from two powerful and hostile families could love each other. The catastrophe from the Titanic recreates a forbidden love between a girl from high society and a humble man.

There's no doubt, the illegal is attractive and provoking, precisely because it's about crossing the limits. Nevertheless, whereas some prohibitions make sense, there are prohibitions that are just absurd prejudices.

Hiding, living a double life, faking everything... It's very painful to feel attracted to an engaged person or someone that is completely surrendered to God. This happens in fiction, but it's also more common than we believe.

Only the person that lives through this first hand understands that it's a painful and challenging experience. It affects them mentally, physically, socially, spiritually, and it also affects their family.

You can't always be so cautious, you can't always be aware of the person you love. The feeling isn't intellectual and it's not controlled by pushing a button.

The problem isn't what I feel, but
what I do with what I feel.

Love is blind. Sometimes it's insanity that drives it and, sometimes, it's the conscious mind that does it. When the mind drives it, sooner or later, it gets bored. When insanity boosts it, the risky emotions and anxiety show up. That's why life is a continuous dance between insanity and sanity.

Freedom and prohibition

It seems that talking about forbidden love implies a contradiction, because if love implies spontaneity and openness, why should we forbid it?

We talk about something forbidden when there's a betrayal or a principle that has been violated.

For example, a Jewish man getting married with a woman that's not Jewish, for a lot of people out of the religion wouldn't be a problem, but within the religion it is a problem, because it violates the principle about people getting married with someone from the same religion.

What would happen if a girl with dark skin married a man with white skin? Nothing, but traditions say that people with similar skin tones should get married, otherwise people will judge them without any reason.

In front of a forbidden love,
there will always be someone
who'll condemn the decision or get pissed off.

Plenty of times, this prohibition doesn't come from the act itself but a previous commitment, one of the two being a minor, or it may come from social prejudices, such as skin color.

There are things that can make love something forbidden, and these things can be well grounded or not.

In some cases, they come from prejudices, but in other cases they could be pretty justified.

You can't forbid being in love, you can only avoid the illicit acts that passion makes one do.

Resisting would be a real sign of personal dominance and fidelity to promises made. In a forbidden love, refusing to consummate the union would be the sign of true love.

Falling in love, and love

Falling in love is one thing, but loving is another thing, and creating an undressed relationship from daily acts is something totally different. While you don't have any control over falling in love, creating a relationship is a free act that requires two people and, no matter how much we want it, we can't always force it.

Falling in love is allowing the chemicals within our organism to affect us and put us out of this reality. It's a passion that is felt and it passes by. It doesn't last. It's a starter motor that stays switched on for around sixteen months.

> *Loving is going beyond being in love,*
> *into maintaining a commitment*
> *with acts of love.*

It's a decision supported by our body's chemistry. After seven years, we'll have to handle the human spirit and the conviction that relationships are created and maintained with strength, maturity, and one's awareness of reality.

What happens when an attraction you didn't expect shows up, one that you feel you can't control, and it's suddenly out of your hand and things just happened? Aren't there things to respect? Is everything allowed? Is nothing forbidden? The latter is simply impossible, limits should always exist, although you may be asking yourself, "How can I choose to not love?"

Remember the golden rule, "Love is one thing, and what I do with it is something different." We live in a culture that encourages us to be responsible for what we feel and not for what we do, when it should be backwards.

When a husband beats and yells at the man that's with his wife, without asking what they are doing together, we excuse him when he claims he did it because he "loves her."

We put responsibilities on the other people because of what we feel, but we avoid the responsibilities we have regarding what we do with what we feel.

*You can't control what you already feel,
but you're responsible for what
you do with what you feel.*

A forty-five-year-old teacher fell in love with his fourteen-year-old student, he had been married for about twenty-four years and he had four children. A forty-five-year-old person should be responsible for what he does, he shouldn't allow being carried by sexual fascination, adventure, and irresponsibility.

This gentleman was committing a crime, he was betraying his family and hurting a little girl at the same time. That relationship would never be prudent because her brain is still developing and she has a subordinated relationship with her teacher, who she sees as an authority.

Plenty of students "fall in love" with their teacher, but these are childish illusions that don't generate bigger consequences.

The problem remains in what the teacher does. That adult should act with responsibility and maturity. It's not about forgiving or being forgiven, it's about who acts as though this wasn't something serious.

What happens when we don't limit the access to pornography that children can have in their phones or tables? Why do we think it's normal for them to go to dangerous places to dance and consume alcohol using fake IDs?

We're pushing them to live experiences that don't match their ages, forcing them to grow up prematurely.

It's not about determining if this is "good" or "bad," but to pose some simple questions, what sort of reality do these behaviors create? Will they help them grow and become better human beings? Where are we going? How much can the rubber band stretch before snapping?

Limits exist
and these convictions
make me be the person I am.

This temptation generated by desire and what's forbidden could always be present, joined to the pleasure that comes from knowing we're crossing boundaries.

In Genesis, Adam and Even were allowed to eat from all of the trees in the Paradise, except from the Tree of Good and Evil, because if they did it, they'd die.

The Snake told them that they'd be like gods, getting to know good and evil. Eve saw the fruit as tempting and finally ate it. Did she do it because of its tasty appearance, because it was forbidden, or because they would be like gods?

The envy of the Devil,
along with Adam and Eve's pride and disobedience
created a space for evilness in the world.

Pride made them forget that they had everything and the fact that they had to be thankful for living in a paradise. They preferred to disobey God, pretending to be like Him and, in that moment, they were ashamed of their nudity, because up to that point they had lived within acceptance and total innocence.

We have to see ourselves within what we are: none of us is God, so none of us get to decide about the lives of everyone else, about dissolving families, using people for pleasure and being an accomplice to betrayal. Sometimes we don't appreciate the small paradise we live in, we get used to the allowed trees, we don't find any taste in them, and, at the slightest provocation, we want to taste the forbidden fruit that will give us a temporary moment of pleasure and, at the same time, a whole story filled with shame and sorrow.

Temptations don't define us, because, as human beings with free will, we have the power and freedom to choose, that's why we still have responsibility for what we are.

Freedom is not doing what we want without limits, this would be almightiness and only God can do that. Freedom is recognizing our limits and still being able to choose.

Love boost

Love boost works as a magnifying glass that shows the relationship's benefits. generating motivations to achieve a harmonious union, overcoming shortcomings, and seeing the person better than what he or she actually is. We idealize them.

This inspires both people in the relationship to show the best version of themselves, because they know they have to achieve higher virtue levels and become better than what was expected, at least for a while.

With this boost, the first movement can create incredible things, the only thing that's necessary is to use their potential well, because it's a powerful creator of change.

When achieving small victories and proximity in the relationship, everything seems more achievable. Creating a boost requires the couple to have a common vision, so they can recognize themselves as a team and motivate themselves mutually.

Without enthusiasm and faith
in the common vision,
the relationship gets stuck.

Infidelity, failure, breakup...

Cheating on someone breaks a promise with them and with one's own self. Nevertheless, women, as well as men, fall in this questionable habit. Women usually do so due to emotional reasons, they need closeness, recognition, and love, and men look for sex and admiration, although it can be a combination of factors.

The fear of a breakup will always be there. A way to dissolve the fear is to be empathic towards the people that have lived what I fear. At the end of their relationship, one of them said, "The last time I saw her, I felt I finally saw her like she really was."

The person shows himself or herself exactly how they are when they leave, because they don't care about it. Their interest is focused on their next victim. That's how disappointment is expressed by a human being that finds out the masks and disguises that stopped them from knowing who they were living with.

*Reality doesn't forgive lies
nor relationships based
on what it "should" be.*

Disappointment also shows up when we create expectations and we don't know what we can and can't offer.

No one can expect giving a euro and receiving something that costs one hundred euros, and no one would ever believe that that idea can be sustainable.

Relationships imply a balance in this giving and taking that must be beneficial for both people involved. When one of the two receives more than what he or she gives, the relationship gets sick.

There's only one path in which we can recognize pain. Nevertheless, there's another path we should not forget, because in here we are aware and grow up inside so pain don't catch us in its webs. The thing is that we have to act before it's too late.

Anyone that finishes with anything, whether it's a relationship, a business, a contract, or a friendship, is not a failure. This experience is just an unexpected adjustment in the path.

If we could define the term "failure" creatively, it would be exactly this: a change of direction.

Appreciating what we are from the spirit has to do with loving our steps and decisions. When a relationship ends, we have to be thankful and continue our path.

If the relationship achieved its goal, we'll be in a different position and we'll move on towards what's next feeling mostly peace.

The mind is like an insane man that can push us towards depression after a breakup or a failure. We have the freedom to choose his decadent speech that makes us feel sad and awful because of what happened, or we can choose being thankful because everything happened and the relationship achieved its goal.

Chapter 2

The ingredients of an undressed relationship

There are five main ingredients in an undressed relationship that seem like the fingers of our hands. They're able to do many things. These elements act like a magnet attracting well-being and realization.

1. Interest

Getting that person's attention is the first step you need in order to have a relationship. Once you get the attention, you'll generate interest.

Modern men are fighting a war in order to get attention. Continuous stimulation, every single minute, is affecting people's perception, to the point that being seen is a war we must win and all sorts of resources are used for that, from the most superficial ones to the most sophisticated ones.

After the first step, after getting that especial person's attention, you'll need it to remain on you. For that you'll require a really attractive content.

There can be twenty people that have the ideal traits and conditions you're looking for in a couple, but you only focus on one of them, because she or he was the one that got your attention and awoke your interest. Sometimes, it won't be easy to define that unknown factor that that person has, nevertheless, you can't stop looking at him or her, and you can't stop wanting to be with him or her.

It's also important to generate interest when addressing him or her. Remember that relationships are a two-way street. When there's only one way, it'll be about relationships where someone is dominant and someone is submissive, and they aren't healthy whatsoever.

Within you, there are several ideas, expectations, wishes, and mental projections about what your ideal partner is. When you get to know that person, you tend to evaluate if he or she has all of the elements or, at least, the majority of the ones you've decided on. Initially, every attraction is intellectual and very basic.

It's also important that some sort of special chemistry exists to make you feel comfortable with him or her. It's a reaction that can't be defined, it simply affects you and makes you feel good. Sometimes, the other person is the first one to notice that energy.

It's important to evaluate what are these elements you expect from your significant other, and which of them are essential and which are not.

The level of ignorance we have about ourselves and what we want is incredible.

You should be the one that knows the most about you and, for that to happen, you must invest in yourself and dedicate time to getting to know yourself.

It's necessary to know with whom you have lived all this time, and how fulfilled you currently are.

When reflecting about the traits your ideal partner must have, try to also think of the *ones* you should have.

I propose you the following exercise.

- Make a list of traits you wish to find in your significant other, the order is not important right now.
- Classify them in two columns. In one of them write the necessary ones and, in the other one, write the ones you think you could pass by.
- Now, take the list of what you couldn't pass by and rank them, from the most important one to the least.

Plenty of times, this first filter is wrong, because the traits you're looking for won't always be the key to feel special with that person.

You'd be surprised. I know so many people that told me, "I've erased the list of traits that I couldn't pass by and I've found this extraordinary person that today is my wife."

When interest disappears, be sure that the relationship is dying. Interest in a relationship is like breathing. You can hold your breath for a moment, but if you do it for too long, you'll need help or you'll die.

If someone maintains a relationship where there's not enough interest, it'll be like living with a corpse rotting from the inside out. A corpse would have to use plenty of masks and layers to hide the stench of the relationship.

Nevertheless, it'll be so evident that any other person will rapidly notice it. That unpleasant humor is called bitterness and, believe me, other people can see it. Bitterness makes people in the relationship sick, as well as the ones surrounding them.

Just like love can't be disguised, bitterness can't be disguised either. In order to know if a person lives with bitterness, it's enough to look at him or her for five seconds, no matter their fame, possessions, politic position, or family.

It doesn't matter if the person is wearing makeup or perfume, the eyes reflect the bitterness and that's something that can't be hidden.

A skilled observer of bitterness is a child between for and seven years old. If you ask such a child to look at your eyes and tell you if you are bitter or not, they'll tell you frankly and honestly.

2. Benevolence

Benevolence is one of the most important ingredients when strengthening a relationship.

Without it, the relationship will be weak and vulnerable, but if it's present, the relationship's muscles will endure heavier burdens and the body will have an energy that will elevate its info-energy and allow it to develop its talents.

Info-energy is all of the information contained in our particular electromagnetic field, related to our genetic heritage and our individual story, including soul experiences, our ancestors' memories, and even information from the culture we were educated in.

The evidence that reality offers us will give us confidence to move forward with benevolence, because it improves the life of both people in a relationship and it even has benefits in the field where each of one of them work.

Benevolence is that quality level that makes you more attractive to the other people and, in my opinion, the most important ingredient, although a relationship starts with interest.

Many people aren't aware of this and that's why their relationships are in a crisis. They can't even define the term properly, so, how can we ask them to practice it every day?

I'll start by asking you the same question I ask everyone that comes to my Undressed Relationship Workshop. "What does benevolence mean to you?"

They give an answer like this, "feeling empathy towards the other person," "showing interest for their wellbeing," "being good or kind," "seeing goodness," "living it," "finding satisfaction when serving the other person," etc.

The answer is not as transcendental as the practice. It's very important to not be simply satisfied with words. You need to practice it in your daily life, because the only thing you have is what you practice. Here's my definition:

Benevolence means being able
to think well about your mistakes
and the mistakes of your significant other.

The cost of benevolence may look silly, whereas the benefit of this kind of attitude is being a person easy to get along with, kind, friendly, easy to be loved, a person that's not dominant or possessive.

If I am benevolent, when you make a mistake, my reaction will be kind and understanding. Nevertheless, the secret to becoming benevolent is to be like that towards yourself first.

I'm not going to deny that, in some cases, benevolence may cut both ways. If you practice benevolence and your partner doesn't do it, then the relationship will fail, because one of you will apologize and the other one will punish. That leads to a disequilibrium and ends up hurting the benevolent one, boosting the other one's abuse.

I remember the case of a man that asked his wife to help him with a task that would facilitate his promotion.

— *"Baby, I need you to be pretty and ready for a dinner with my boss that will help me get the promotion I really want. It's at eight thirty in the evening. Please, buy a dress and prepare as though we're going to a wedding."*

The woman had thousands of things to do that day, nevertheless, when applying that benevolence, she decided to say "Yes" without creating drama or exaggerating anything.

When she hung up the phone, she felt the burden of responsibility. She had to postpone several appointments and make one at a beauty salon and, on top of that, she had to go shopping, because she was pregnant so she didn't have dresses to wear.

She was really busy the whole day, but she finally got to do everything she had to do. When it was eight thirty, she felt happy, because she was ready. She sat in her living room, thinking,

— *"I'm ready and on time. This time I'll surprise you, because I won't make you wait."*

It was a quarter to nine and her husband hadn't called her nor arrived. She could have made a dramatic scene, behaved like a victim, or even become very aggressive, but, with benevolence, she said:

— *"Surely, he has something important to do, so he can't call me and that's why he hasn't come yet."*

It was nine o'clock when she called him, but he didn't reply and he didn't come, either. This created a higher level of discomfort and, therefore, a bigger burden to benevolence. She knew the terms of the relationship she wanted to create with her significant other. If she got angry and made any sort of drama, it could have affected her relationship and that wasn't what she wanted. So she decided to exclaim,

— *"I'm still ready, ah!"*

It was ten in the evening when her husband arrived in the car and whistling, instead of getting in the house.

She found the undressed reality moment.

—*"I'm still ready,"* she said while walking towards the car.

She opened the door and looked at her husband in the eyes. His face was happy, but at the same time he was worried by the reaction she would have because he had arrived very late.

Letting go of what just happened, she said:

— *"Baby, I know your dinner was successful and you certainly had important reasons why you weren't able to call me, but I bought a party dress and you surely received your promotion, so tell me where you're going to take me to, because this beauty deserves to go out to a special place with the love of her life."*

If I ask any man, "Who would want a partner like this?" all of them would answer affirmatively. This is a couple with benevolence.

On the other hand, women would say: "She's an idiot! She's going to be a fool every day. She had to make a scene so he would be afraid and realize what had to be done. If necessary, she would need to find what hurts him the most and tell him that that's what she's going to do... Leave him without sex one week, don't make him dinner, stop ironing his shirts... Anything to make him feel pain!"

Now, I'll include an example of a benevolent man, so women don't feel benevolence is just for them.

An executive was married with a woman trader and they had a mutual agreement that said that she could spend no more than 1,700 dollars with the credit card every month.

So, every month, the bank statement showed amounts like 1,700 dollars, there were times in which the amount was 1,550 dollars, other times when it was 1,720 dollars, and everything was stable in their relationship.

On a good day, the executive received his credit card bank statement and he found the amount of 17,400 dollars spent by his wife.

He thought:

— *"How could my wife spend 17,400 dollars this month without telling me anything?"*

But then, he decided to act with benevolence.

— *"Before calling her, screaming, and complaining, I'm going to think she must have had a valid and important reason for spending that amount of money."*

The husband waited to arrive at home to ask her the question in person, so he could be in control and avoid making any Shakespearian drama, because the only result would from it would be death.

When seeing his wife, he said, "Baby, I got the bank statement and it says that someone spent 17,400 dollars. First, I want to know if you did that."

— *"Yes,"* she answered.

— *"I can imagine that you had a very important reason to spend that amount of money and I respect that, so I wish to ask you what sort of strategy you have in order to pay that amount of money, because the card interests are high."*

If I ask you ladies, "How many of you would like to have a husband like that?" Surely all of you would raise your hands. But if I asked the men, "How would you evaluate this husband's behavior?" You'll surely tell me that "he's an idiot and surely she'll continue abusing him." That's the cost of benevolence.

The modern human being doesn't establish undressed relationships because they are the result of living with benevolence. Here, romantic love definitions don't matter, nor the "correct" roles or the "expected" reactions of what you can accept or not.

This is the secret of an undressed relationship that improves this reality and that actually makes us more human and less intellectual.

It's an act that implies an inner strength that not many human beings can have with their partners and it shows eternal appreciation.

Benevolence must have a balance so it doesn't create frustration or abuse, like we just said. It must be reciprocal, a two-way thing, therefore, it must become a subject of daily conversations.

Human beings make mistakes every day
and we need benevolence to be better.

Every time I talk about this, people find it very difficult to get through it, because it's about an attitude that's not contemplated in modern education. This shows how far away from the ingredients that create a long-term relationship we really are.

Perhaps, that's why we have a high rate of relationships that don't las. Take it into consideration if you want to obtain good results in your relationship.

3. Identity

The third element of undressed relationships is identity. It consists in not losing your value, despite having a complete and whole relationship that makes you feel fulfilled.

Sometimes, people merge in a relationship and they end up leaving their identity behind in order to satisfy their partner. When this happens, the relationship is just an appearance, without any conflict, completely forgetting that there are two different realities within the relationship as well.

In these cases, the bond seems stable because it becomes comfortable, but it dies when losing one of its members, and then it'll lose the other one, too. When erasing the identity becomes a pattern, one of the two stops being present in the relationship, although she or he continues being physically there.

Relationships imply alterity:
it's the union of two different but
complementary individuals.

One thing is being benevolent, a different thing is erasing one's personality. Curiously, the ones that rebel before benevolence are able to erase themselves in a relationship, therefore they don't seize the most important ingredient, benevolence, and they also fail at another crucial one, identity.

Sometimes, the person erases himself or herself and there are other times in which they let themselves be erased. The absence of respect is the worst that someone can have. If everything in the relationship is about trying to change the other person so he or she can be adjusted to a preconceived idea, or to break himself or herself to adapt the other person's expectations, the weariness that results from this will be fatal.

Whether we like it or not, this life is lived in solitude and it's developed in the relationship.

Only from the authenticity of an undressed
relationship can we be healthily fulfilled.

This is the big challenge, to develop ourselves with the other person, without stopping being ourselves and celebrating that the other person can be himself or herself too. It's a mystery and a challenge to achieve that goal.

4. Integrity

The fourth element of an authentic relationship is integrity, and it's rooted in freedom and coherence. It implies that I am one, alone, and complete, and I'm not divided nor hidden.

Integrity is the result of incorporating values in my life, owning them, and practicing them. I can express my worth when I am with my significant other, and that gives every relationship a superior dimension.

If you want your integrity to have an impact in the relationship, you must live with coherence. If you feel and think A, you say A, and act with A. Coherence strengthens your integrity. Your emotional, mental, and even physical health is the evidence that you live with integrity and coherence.

To be integral, I need to know who I am
and dare to live the experience of being myself.

It's very important to have the ability to laugh at oneself and allow the other people to laugh at you. This is an act of humbleness and integrity, because only when I stop taking myself too seriously, will I be myself with authenticity, without pretending to be something I am not.

Being confident is the key to showing yourself undressed without looking for external validation. The best validation comes from experiencing your inner values. Your value isn't in what you look like, but in what you are and what you do. When you live as an integral person with another person that is also integral, you can experience how they add value to their lives.

In relationships, there's a limit that isn't negotiable and that's precisely your integrity.

What you are, what you believe, your worth, what makes your life meaningful are all aspects that can't be negotiated. Even when a conflict shows up, it's preferable to face it before losing one's integrity.

If you don't place limits, and you negotiate your integrity, you'll be dying in your relationship and you'll feel you're losing your life and your worth. There will be a moment when you will stop feeling interest and respect for the bond, that's why it's better to end it as soon as possible, instead of accumulating pain, frustration, and failure.

If your relationship doesn't allow you to live with integrity, you could get sick and it could become a chronic condition. Maybe you gave one of your principles or convictions up to satisfy that person or maybe you did something together you are both ashamed of.

You can always go from shame to integrity through forgiveness and hope.

5. Add value to my reality

The level of frustration you feel will indicate the level of value the relationship gives you. The bigger the frustration is, the smaller the value. If your relationship is feeding and adding value to your reality, then the fifth element is satisfied.

Another way to know if it adds value is your level of energy. The vitabytes become a magnet that attracts abundance and fulfillment, this is the big power the fifth ingredient has in an undressed relationship.

If the relationship is healthy and it helps both parties grow up, this will be reflected in other areas of life.

When a relationship becomes mediocre
or isolates you from family and
friends, that's a warning.

Other indicators that you can analyze to know if your relationship adds value to your reality are:

* **Goodbye ego:** To add value in the relationship, one must put prejudices aside and go to a different level. When each one of us puts our ego and its products (power, control, comparison, jealousy, envy) aside, then what's left is an undressed relationship in which each one of you shows up like what you really are, improving the value consciously. This process of self-

discovery becomes a concert with sound, images, and lights that transform us drastically and positively, elevating our life voltage.

• **The "perfect" couple:** You should never follow your enemy's advice, but, sometimes, you shouldn't follow your friend's advice either. This also applies to what society says, because society loves shapes, mind, and what's right, but dislikes people living however they want.

There's a hidden desire
to control the other people.

Whether it's disguised envy, a need to be part of other people's lives and manipulate them, or to pretend to be useful, in any case, control always implies violating the other person's freedom.

When two people do everything this society dictates to be the "perfect" couple, they end up in a perfect breakup, and in a perfect frustrating mood, of course, with society's approval.

They create a model, a "should be" that seems to be above all and it doesn't matter if, in order to achieve it, people end up profoundly unhappy. However, to remain in that mood, they' have to lie to themselves and fake joy.

- **Lies and illness:** When reality is a big lie generated by our mind, the body gets the attention back with an illness. Those who live in their relationship feeling inferior, an illness visits them in the shape of a mental or emotional affliction. Those who still feel guilty are affected by tiredness and depression, the ones who live with fear present articulation and breathing problems, and those who can't handle hate tend to have heart troubles or even develop cancer.

  Although plenty of illnesses are presented by other factors, most of the times they happen due to externalized conflicts generated by our actions and lies.

  The body doesn't lie. An unhappy person will end up sick. Before the evidence of an illness, one must act, but the best is to not wait for illness to show up.

*The important thing is to hear your body
and read the signs that it sends you.*

- **Assertiveness and clear rules:** It's very important for you to learn to negotiate with your partner. Allow them to be how they want to be and, at the same time, you should try to be yourself. For that, you'll need creativity, because you'll have to look for the best practices to not disappear nor impose yourself in a way where only your own interests and decisions are important. The key is to have clear rules about what's allowed and what's not within a relationship. These would be a life jacket when things get tough and you feel you're losing your minds.

In an undressed relationship, the cheerful and harmonic moments should be appreciated and you be thankful for it, and be filled with tenderness for the person with us. This way, you'll have emotional energy with you wherever tiredness, routine, time, family, and the influences of your friends, bosses, or coworkers affect the relationship. These influences will bring you to a difficult level for the couple. Avoiding obstacles will require talent, patience, creativity, and the ability to negotiate. This is important in achieving a real relationship that both of you appreciate. The ideal thing is no more than seven rules, so they can be easy to remember and you both must reevaluate them constantly to see if they work or if they should be modified.

*It's always better to have awful rules
than not having rules at all.*

The mere practice of including each one's requests will help both of you know your interests, priorities, and worries. This will give you order and a frame of reference. I always say that order is for those who feel fragile and want to take care of themselves, but disorder is the luxury of those who aren't afraid of losing time, health, money, effort, and a life partner as well.

- **Being independent:** Taking care of each one's identities is something more powerful than respect, it's deeper and it goes beyond it, because it implies actively defending what each one of you are. "I respect my identity and yours and we both maintain respect in the relationship." It's a balance between independency and interdependency.

Authenticity and autonomy are
defended within the relationship.

Interdependency is being together without depending on each other. You are both self-sufficient, you can express anything without adapting to the other person, the environment, or social rules. When a relationship is interdependent, three **basic and strengthening actions** are achieved, actions known as the "Three Cs," you are **convenient** as a couple, you **contain** yourself when being weak, and you know how to **content** with the other person when going through a fight.

- **Why did you break up:** Being with your partner should add something to your life. If your relationship isn't adding anything, then you're getting worse and you should evaluate if you want to continue.
Life is just a fraction of time, allow yourself to do with it something wonderful and not simply an experience to fill other people's expectations.
When you break up with your significant other, people ask why you guys broke up and they always hope to

hear an awful reason. Nevertheless, I've never heard someone asking, "Why did you guys move on?"

Sometimes, there's not a specific reason to break up, sometimes there are only reasons to move on and that's it.

* **Self-sabotage:** Many people that, at heart, don't wish to stop being single, sabotage themselves when there's an opportunity to meet a potential partner.

  Sometimes, not only do they refuse the opportunity to go out, but also, with their behavior, people don't want to talk to them anymore. For example, when you talk negatively about your dates or previous relationships, you despise your own aspect or intelligence, or when you express yourself with pessimist attitudes, especially about the opposite sex, and you find something to criticize in the first minutes of the conversation.

The best recipe to get to know your significant other is being honest and showing yourself exactly like you are.

Another way to self-sabotage can be arriving late, inventing excuses, showing yourself extremely available and reacting with rejection and shame towards their answer, etc.

This can be fought by being willing to meet new people, but you have to be yourself, with the whole confidence you can get to transmit.

It doesn't matter how many qualities we look for in a partner if, at heart, we don't wish them; subconsciously, we'll look for coherence regarding our search for a partner, therefore, the romance will end sooner or later if the partner doesn't have the qualities we look for.

This way, the best thing you can do is to be honest. If you find out that you really want to establish that relationship, commit to maintaining that bond.

- **Good sense of humor:** Our closest people become our mirror. We get to know ourselves through them and, most of the time, we don't like what we see, this is a very hard and painful experience, because it makes us discover dark and unpleasant things about ourselves. Seeing our inner gorilla and learning to love him is the mission we all have.

A good sense of humor
is a very important ingredient.

The person who doesn't learn to laugh at the prehistoric being that generates an influence in the decisions that puts them in trouble will have a really bad time. That Neanderthal will tell you to follow the weakest law: don't do anything productive, dedicate yourself to losing time, play with your phone looking for likes in your social media, eat everything you want... Taking everything too seriously generates problems in relationships.

- **Approach:** This isn't only a positive thinking, it's a tangible reality from the **Wise Being** we all have inside. What ends shows a change of direction, it adds life to your life, and it creates a new experience that will surely be enriching, although the first step for this could be a bit difficult or stormy.

What's new produces fear
to the mind that looks for control.

It's important to learn how to trust yourself and that life won't give you problems you can't overcome.
When the problem is too big, you look carefully. Life tends to put you near the people and the resources you need so you can use them and grow up.
Remember that, in order to flourish, life prunes us, removing the dried parts, what can't breathe anymore, before they affect our healthy parts, because this won't do us any good.
Life has its falls that removes our dried leaves, learn to enjoy this season that prepares you for being reborn in the spring.

- **Failure as a trampoline:** Failure has a benefiting and valuable consequence, it makes you go back to your heart and it invites you to look within yourself.
Here's when people focus, invest time and resources on themselves again. This is the starting point that can lead to success.

A very old story tells that a man found a chest filled with treasures, but when opening it, he didn't see anything and threw it away, without realizing that the chest was the treasure itself. That's how failure works, it seems like it doesn't have anything good, but it's actually the gas that pushes us to move forwards with more energy. Hormones like endorphins and adrenaline help us overcome adversities, allowing us to discover the hidden treasures behind any failure.

Great treasures disguised as failures
drove us to the success we enjoy today.

The ability to preserve our true treasures makes us humans and it elevates us spiritually, because it makes us great people and, at the same time, it teaches us to become humble.

The transforming power of relationships

There is a huge transforming power in a relationship where people look at life in motion and in an undressed way, being cheered up by their improvements. The people who get related in an undressed way inspire peace and help the people surrounding them develop their talents in a harmonious way, showing a life energy that manifests in health which makes them tremendously attractive.

We all can build and maintain
an undressed relationship.

This type of relationships has a tremendous healing potential filled with abundance and happiness, which are essential to achieving fulfillment, allowing you to be conscious of your wounds and the fact that you need to heal them yourself, motivating you to grow, improve, and discover yourself.

It'll be convenient to learn first what an undressed relationship consists of, and then you get committed to it. Commitment helps the undressed relationship last and it makes it work in the most stable way, like railroads.

Perhaps, you'll find out that a relationship represents a big challenge. However, if you do your job well, you'll see the results. You'll notice an inner boost that will make you take the risk and practice it.

What men expect from women

The five things a man expects from a woman in the frame of a relationship are like your toes—although you don't see them, they support you in order to walk. For some men, the list can change, but it's important to start from the basic parts as a reference point.

* **Touch and not an emotional hit:** First, I want to clarify that every act you do or don't do is caught by the other person as a touch or an emotional hit. If you learn to read the way your acts are seen by your significant other, you'll find out how he or she feels about your actions so you'll be accountable regarding what you add or subtract to his or her life.

* **Sex:** A friend is a person that shows you appreciation with acts. When he or she doesn't do it, your brain interprets it as a punch that damages the relationship.

  A partner is a person that, beyond appreciating you and showing you that appreciation with acts, she or he has a relationship with you that goes to sexual intimacy in a wide sense, beyond the genital parts.

  In fact, in order to get to the sexual relationship, one must go through romanticism, sensuality, provocation, eroticism, arousal, and then the genitals, to reach subtlety the final touch.

  This should be considered based on two quality indicators: quantity and quality. Nevertheless, it can't be forced nor asked through blackmailing, because it'll diminish its essence, meaning, and satisfaction.

  It also can't have conditions, because you'll fall in an emotional prostitution and it'll end up making you unhappy, becoming a seed for infidelity and suffering in the couple, or it can also be the end of the relationsh p.

The essence of an undressed relationship
is improving the reality
of both people in a tangible way.

If you're a guy, understand that women go through periods that, although they love you, they don't want sex every time nor immediately, and the seduction part will require a bigger effort.

She'll have to make an effort too, in order to be more accessible and understand the big importance sex has for her partner, although, for her, that isn't in her five priorities.

The subject of sex is complex.

Here, we mention what sex implies in an undressed relationship. It's a series of acts where spirits connect, generating a higher bond, am improvement of reality in all sorts of aspects enhancing a lovely and understanding environment.

- **Company:** It implies presence, something that's felt, and it works as a touch, never as a punch. It's getting close without invading, presence without judgment.
  Since the beginning, men have always required a partner.

Having company isn't a vigilant presence judging, asking, and requiring. Sensibility is required to identify what the other person needs in the relationship, and when to give it to him or her. It seems complicated, but it isn't. You simply need to practice attention and empathy.

Company is being attentive at the moment and willing to give company when it's required. When there's anger or that person simple wants space, you have to hold back, but if you both spend too much time in your business, on tablets or phones, the relationship gets cold because you don't share anymore.

You both should do the work. If you're a woman, your man must be the first priority, before your children, your parents, your friendships, or your job.

This is one of the points that generates the biggest conflicts for women in a relationship.

Normally, they don't agree and rebel, forgetting a small detail: this temporary life isn't intellectual and what matter is what works and not what the mind believes.

Make your partner the first priority,
this is essential to maintaining
the relationship alive.

In this sense, Evidence-Based Execution will help you avoid plenty of headaches. This practice is fundamental in my workshops and it's about "giving evidence of what's found" by applying the ideas I share, extracted from my experience with reality.

When I am asked why a relationship ended, the answer is very simple: because the two parties decided that that didn't work.

The "should be" theoretical approach doesn't work in the real world. Relationships, and especially romantic relationships, are a source of mental, physical, and spiritual health. I invite you to live an undressed relationship with your partner and learn what works and what doesn't work.

+ **The "other" family:** Put aside the "family is first" idea, referring to one's family of origin. There are hospitals that separate the patient from his or her "family" for months so the patient will recover from the emotional aggressions, the criticisms, and the judgment that he or she receives from his or her "loved ones."

Sometimes, family limits our growth, because it doesn't accept that you get out of the flowerpot where you were planted. Many of your goals are blocked by the strength of the limits generated in your own house. When you're in a relationship, it's fundamental to remember that this is now your family and not the one you were born in.

If your family affects your relationship negatively, you should establish clear limits and make conscious decisions, because their conditioning continues, even if you're an adult.

What's really worthwhile in a family
is the quality of the relationship,
and not just the blood bonds.

You can create harmony, kindness, understanding, peace, inclusion, and even respect, in the relationships with the people that carry the same last name with you.

A valuable family is the one that makes authentic acts filled with company and concern about you.

• **Appearance:** Normally, guys are very visual, and they want their partners to look pretty for them. Appearance is your personal image and, as such, it should project what you are, but it also has to be nice for the ones around you.

Men look first and then let appearances affect them, but, afterwards, they discover the content. That's why a woman that doesn't take care of herself, that shows up messy, reflects the little interest she has in her male partner and, without noticing, she's allowing everyone to see their relationship is in trouble.

When you go to a big party, you get dressed up in a beautiful dress and you invest some time in the beauty salon. The guests become the protagonists and they are photographed for their appearance, which is a way to say thanks to the person who invited them. A woman that looks pretty, shows that she's having fun in her relationship. Someone loves her, desires her, and motivates her to look stunning.

When a woman looks pretty and doesn't have a couple, it's an evidence she has an excellent relationship with herself and also demonstrates her great personal value.

Surely, she'll have several options but she won't take them without first considering them.

We are deep and have a shape,
which is our appearance,0
and it must show what's inside.

◆ **Admiration:** This is a difficult point because admiration is subjective. A man could feel pretty awful when he's not admired at home.

The man is fragile regarding his emotional structure and he requires his partner's support to feel valuable, nevertheless, it's the partner that normally criticizes him, although she does it with good intentions.

A man feels safe when he has his partner's admiration.

Admiration makes him make huge decisions that reinforce the subjective feeling that becomes way more objective, achieving goals in the financial, emotional, and social aspects.

If the man doesn't feel that his woman admires him, he won't be able to create wealth for her. When admiration is absent, complaints, problems, and grudges show up that end up becoming unbearable.

On the other hand, when there's admiration from the woman towards the man, a deep harmony is present in the relationship.

Showing admiration is a continuous habit that supports development and goals, and it solidifies the union.

◆ **Taking care of the house and children:** Whether we like it or not, men have the hunter instinct and women are better administrators and caretakers. Although these roles have changed by social and economic requirements or by mere conviction, nature hasn't changed. For a man, it's very important that the woman should know how to take care of children, so they grow up and become independent. This doesn't imply that she should only do that task, nevertheless, she shouldn't evade it, because it's a natural law.

In modern marriages that have inverted these roles, this still works, but now the woman is the one that hunts and bring home resources, while the man takes care of the house and the children.

Here, the thing is that the guy doesn't feel out of his

place because he's doing that, and the woman shouldn't feel superior because she's bringing home the money. When mer went to war, women moved on alone.

It'll always be very positive for a smart woman to contribute with sustaining the family that man and woman carry.

It's about teamwork.

What women expect from men

* **Attention:** A woman expects a man to give her affection, tenderness, and mostly, attention. Nevertheless, men don't put too much effort in that, because they think women are very demanding, always asking for things, when women only want them to focus on one specific thing: attention just for a minute.

  Attention is shown with every sense. Women feel valued when men dedicate unlimited time to listen to them, when women aren't interrupted nor questioned. They tend to think when speaking, so they need to express themselves to achieve clarity regarding what they need.

One of the biggest complaints women have of their men is that they don't feel men listen to them.

When you listen, you let the other person express themselves fully, without interruptions, putting attention not only to the content, but also to the feelings.

You listen when you're able to repeat the most important parts with precision; when you answer what you are asked and you put all of your attention on the speech again; when you maintain visual contact and react with empathy regarding their emotions and gestures; when you know how to end the conversation with a smile, a hug, a touch, or a kiss.

Attention with your eyes: This type of attention is easier for a guy because guys are more visual. It's shown when you notice she has a different makeup, new shoes, a new haircut, when you recognize the house is clean or with new ornaments.

*Your eyes allow you to put attention
on the details that make people's lives meaningful.*

It's a huge gift for a woman to get her partner to recognize what he sees, to say it with words, and to appreciate it.

Attention with your touch: The touch is really important for women. We must be aware of the kind of touch we give them. You can't touch them the same way you touch a friend. It's also important to be cozy in the mattress they use, the couch where they read. These things are pure love for the relationship.

Attention with smells: Smell is something key for women. A guy should, besides being clean for her, always smell good. Taking care of odors is essential because passions wakes up or leaves due to the smells.

One of the main attractive traits of a man is his smell, because his body has a certain odor that attracts or pushes away a woman. There's nothing more attractive for a woman that a man with a nice smell and who also knows how to make her smile and relax.

*Good sense of humor is one
of the best perfumes a man can have.*

Attention with flavors: The taste the other people perceive from us can be bitter or sweet, it may be salty or acidic, with different tones. It's key to understand that the way you live generates a flavor. If your words, actions, and emotions had a taste, what would they be?

♦ **Knowing how to appreciate:** Making a woman feel appreciated is essential for the relationship. Nevertheless, it's sometimes hard for her to perceive compliments as something real. Their mental complexity makes them question her partner's words and she may consider them exaggerated.
It's something that can't be generalized, but you'll need to put a lot of attention in it. Women change, the

way they feel recognized will do so too, it's a mystery you'll have to attend to. The level of difficulty doesn't make it less important, you'll have to find the keys yourself.

* **Trust:** Trust is the foundation of a relationship, but if you try to grab it, it'll leave. A woman can tell you that she trusts you, but her trust is volatile. Because of her nature, she'll mistrust her significant other, sooner or later. This forces you to be prepared for any given situation.

The level of trust you have towards the other people reflects the level of trust you have towards yourself.

Accept the level of trust you receive and, if you wish for it to be higher, show with actions that it can be so. There's the generalized perception that men lie and of course it's true, we're all imperfect human beings and we lie once in a while.

When men try to flirt with women through their words, they tend to exaggerate. When it comes to women, they try to flirt with their image, so they use makeup or filters on their social media.

Nevertheless, when it comes to a relationship, men and women should have the same level of sincerity and trust.

* **Money:** Being able to maintain a house is another important element that a woman expects from a man. When the man isn't able to provide something to the table, problems will show up.

  There are several social classes, but as long as you spend money based on the social class you're in right now, then you'll have everything under control.

  If you belong to a lower class, spend like it, the same happens if belong to a middle class.

  You must always be clear regarding your reality. Problems start when you belong to a middle class and you want to spend as though you belonged to a higher class. You get in debt and end up with emotional problems and concerns that will seriously affect your relationship.

* **Genes:** The fifth element a woman focuses on in order to consider a man attractive is that he should be healthy so she can have children with good genetics. This is something they don't say, but this has a huge weight subconsciously, because it determines their future and that of their descendants.

  If you play a sport, eat healthy, and have an athletic body, you tend to be more attractive. This element makes her, without realizing, examine your family's health.

  It seems meaningless, but it's more important than you think.

I know couples that haven't gotten married because the woman found some illness that could affect her children's future. This is the part that's related to health, but it's also important the looks. A tall and strong man, with a masculine face, and attractive hands will have more success with women through an unconscious instinct to preserve the species.

Finding or building

It's not your fault if you haven't found a long-term relationship, but it's your responsibility to do the necessary things to build it, if that's what you wish. If you have had problems several times, that's not a reason to give up.

The answer isn't outside, in our apartment, our ideal job or partner, the key is recognizing our own freedom and ability to give in to our selfishness, so we can make changes and assume responsibilities.

To summarize, it's about trying to start a journey towards your own maturity, and if you're doing it with a partner, he or she should make the journey happier.

If you wish to look for a long-term and complete relationship seriously, you have to be that serious when being single. Essentially there are four steps that can be useful before your partner shows up and starts on the journey of the undressed relationship with you:

+ educate yourself about what undressed, honest, authentic, and mature relationships are,
+ work on your self-awareness deeply, as no one else should know more about you than yourself,
+ practice your abilities by forming healthy relationships with real people, and
+ improve your behaviors and your coping mechanisms that stop you from maintaining a relationship as much as you can.

If it starts within you, in your inner house, you won't have so many difficulties finding a couple that can assume a commitment with you, and he or she probably won't frustrate you.

I propose that you take the time to work on yourself first. This doesn't mean you can't go out with anyone, quite the opposite! Your current relationships constitute an ideal field of preparation.

What I mean is that you should postpone a commitment if you still aren't ready. Fix your singleness now, don't wait for another breakup. Becoming a conscious single person prepares you for the mutual awareness adventure of an undressed relationship.

An undressed relationship gets refreshed
by the continuous interests both members have
when getting to know each other without any fear.

This is the level of trust you both should have. It's a spiritual act that the mind isn't able to do.

When preparing to start any trip, it's important to know how the field is. To organize a trip with someone else, you have to know a lot about yourself, about the other person, and his or her relationships as well.

Unconscious choice

Choosing our partner is, in so many ways, a product of our unconscious, which has its own agenda, and what it wishes is to heal past wounds that we haven't healed yet.

For this purpose, it creates a detailed image of an appropriate partner, and this partner is sought through the appropriate chemistry.

And what is this chemistry? It's just the unconscious attraction we experience towards someone, because we have the sensation he or she will make our emotional, social, and spiritual desires come true. Specifically, we look forward to satisfying the desire we have of healing our past deficiencies.

These wounds require understanding, patience, clarity, honest and humble expressions of pain and abandonment in order to be healed.

We pretend to cover our past deficiencies, but in truth, none of us succeed. In fact, perhaps, we can't even fulfil our own desires, because this isn't the real essence of a relationship.

Living with ambiguity and feeling incomplete drives you towards humbleness and puts your ego in its place, so you become someone easier to live with.

Your undressed relationship should show that you can become a transparent person for yourself and for her or him.

Your foundations

We all have invisible structures within us, those are our foundations, these are built through the interaction with our past needs, how they were attended back then, and how this was carved in our unconsciousness.

We live wishing to find what we didn't have in our past relationships. When we find a person that fills these needs, chemistry is produced and the idea that makes you go to him or her is activated. "**I like him or her, he or she attracts**

me, I'm interested." The rest of the notions of what you wish to find in a person are discarded, you don't evaluate if he or she has this or that trait anymore, even if they were indispensable in your intellectual list.

We feel alive and complete. We are sure we found the person that will fix everything. Unfortunately, it's probable that we chose someone with negative traits like the ones that hurt us in our past relationships. Therefore, we're very likely to have a very awful result in this case.

In fact, most of the people that have had serious relationships claim that, despite having had the best intentions, they managed to find the same problems over and over again.

If our behavior when searching for a partner isn't connected to our current reality, we're doomed to fail, both when it comes to finding a partner as well as maintaining a relationship.

Chapter 3

Undressed relationships with everything and everyone

Hurt people harm others, healthy people heal. Knowing we are healthy is a blessing for the people surrounding us. When you take care of yourself and you start working in order to solve everything that's hurting within you, you become a valuable and nourishing person for everybody.

Not only does getting along with you get easier, but you also heal the souls of other people, because someone who's getting healed is a living example and possesses such a high energy level that it heals everyone around by his or her resonance.

We think we observe the other people, but we are almost always projecting on them our beliefs, imaginations, and inner expectations. This is an obstacle for undressed relationships with friends and partners. We only form an inner relationship within the MIND THAT LIES and, when we see the truth, we get disappointed.

Relationships are vibrations. If you don't vibe, you don't resonate with the other people. It's all about natural vibrations, not intellectual ones. A relationship is an exchange enriched with information that isn't going to be destroyed and that, if it becomes conscious, it improves our reality.

Normally, healing energy is so noticeable that it's perceived immediately. People feel that time flies and that they had a good time whenever they spend time with you.

It's shown that undressed relationships are nourishing, and they work to heal illnesses. Sometimes, the best medicine can be a visit of a friend that, with his or her sympathy, simplicity, and joy, cheers us up and gives us the patience to continue fighting.

These are some of the effects that an undressed relationship with high energy produces:

- it generates a sensation of well-being,
- it helps reduce physical pain,
- it reduces cortisol levels, the stress hormone,
- it reduces the risk to catch colds, develop infections, immunological and cardiovascular problems, and
- if there's cancer, it helps you follow the treatment with better results.

The deeper relationships are, the more they benefit our intellectual, physical, and spiritual health. Scientific Report magazine from Oxford University published that maintaining solid friendships produces endorphins, and these induce a bigger analgesic effect than medicine. Beyond well-being, endorphins enhance bonds, that's why we aren't surprised the levels of this hormone are so altered when there is clinical depression, which partially explains why depressed people can't find pleasure and get isolated.

We are social animals
and we have evolved to live in a group.

The maturity, depth, quality, and quantity of our social relationships affect our physical and mental health, and it even affects our longevity.

Nowadays, the media enhance virtual relationships managed by the **Mind that Lies**. We tend to lie regarding what we say about ourselves, because, even if we try to be objective, we wouldn't make it.

Only in this reality, through cohabitation, other people will get to know us how we really are. But, the opinion they have about us isn't under our control or distance, unless we ask them and see if they have the same trust in order to transmit it.

For that, our enemies are very useful, because they tell us clearly every negative thing they think about us, and reveal that shadow we project on every real human being.

This reflection is an invitation to prioritize real friends. Those are the rules that can help us the most in order to achieve the well-being of a long lasting, happy, and healthy life.

Being who we are

Working with a group of parents in Panamá, a very pretty lady with long hair and lipstick asked me:

— *"Why, if we know we are valuable, is it so hard to live it? Why can't we just be ourselves? Why being authentic in our relationships is so difficult?"*

— *"Good question!" I told her happily.*

Being ourselves seems so difficult for us and we struggle when being what we are because we don't dare explore our talents and define our dreams. We prefer to achieve someone else's expectations, adjusting ourselves to molds we were given since we were children, because this makes us feel safe.

The answer comes from our childhood and culture. From the moment you were born, you have learned a series of habits at home. Perhaps your parents, seeing such a hostile world, taught you to be a likeable person, someone that wants to be loved by the other people. They trained you to look for the validation of others.

That way, everyone helps you and nobody hurts you—or at least that's what you think. In English, it's called **the price of nice**, the price you pay to be agreeable, which is very high, by the way.

They taught you manners, to do what the other people ask, to not step out the line, to avoid bad words, to satisfy the other people, to achieve what everyone expects from you, to say **"yes"** to other people even if you want to say **"no,"** to avoid the truth when it's offensive, to adapt to the needs of everyone else and push yours aside.

You learned to avoid your authenticity, because it shocked others, to do what everyone does to be included and accepted, to not break any society habit so you can be part of it, and then, after a while, this whole thing became a habit as well.

Nevertheless, sooner or later, you get to a point where frustration forces you to rebel, although that rebellion costs you the rejection from a society that used to clap for you. You need a huge inner strength to dare get out of the mold and continue through a path that you chose to be who you really are.

This effort will generate plenty of conflicts, because if you make it, other people in your society will want to do the same, and this would be a problem for every single group.

You'll have to move forwards despite your frustration and the obstacles people around you will put before you. This is one of the reasons why being ourselves is so difficult, because not all of us are willing to risk so much. You're only able to assume this challenge when your spiritual food nurtures you and gives you the resources to comprehend your worth, when you allow yourself to be who you are and feed yourself with inner energy to compensate for everything you received before from the outside, from society.

Now, you will feel energy and satisfaction when developing your talents and contributing something to this humanity.

Being yourself and allowing your significant other to be who she or he is, represents the biggest challenge in an undressed relationship.

Integrating individuality

You don't need to go against everything and everyone to be yourself, you don't need to abandon commitments or people for a sudden idea. Balance comes when you understand that no one lives alone in this life, and that forces you to learn how to work in a team.

You're a unique individual, but in order to stay with the other people, sometimes you need to willingly and humbly give your perspective up. In a community filled with respect, as a family, a team, or a company, you can expose your ideas, but at the end, one must decide what's the best for everyone.

This is healthy and valid, because it strengthens the group's identity and that of each one of the individuals. Being a leader that integrates and respects each participant's individuality is very important so it results in the reality enhancing the common good.

Projections and lies

The enemy is inside. Don't look for enemies outside, it's you and your intellectual gorilla who put you in a harder situation with everybody and everything.

You have a memory that stores information from something you believe you lived, when, in fact, those are just interpretations. One thing is having lived something, and something totally different is what you remember.

Painful memories contain an intellectual dose that wasn't true, but our memory recorded it as something true and it's able to bet that it happened like that.

The brain stores fake scenarios
and firmly believes that they happened like that.

In its inner structure, the mind leans to think that it's right. Finally, it's designed to survive, not to say the truth. If it has to lie to you or to itself so you can survive, that's what it will do.

That's why there are so many prisoners that think they're innocent, politicians that justify their abuse of power, or couples that, before a breakup, blame each other.

The lies about the memories that hurt us can be healed using a new mood for the same situation. You can't erase a memory, but you can record another one on top of the one that was hurtful in order to eliminate it.

This new interpretation of what could have happened allows you to get rid of the pain that what your mind thinks is the only thing that could have happened.

You can become your own therapist when observing your painful memories from different perspectives, without drama.

You can't change the past, but you can change your mind's interpretation of the past. If this new interpretation is made from a mood of peace, you could heal almost any emotional wound that's stopping you from being yourself in the present.

In order to make this transformation, you need to be well, you require plenty of vitabytes that allow you to reprogram your core.

This memory change can't be done with only words. You need inner energy in order to put your brain in a healing state.

We'll be in control when healing our wounds if we get a bigger clarity regarding our interpretations of the past and with the inner energy that we can generate with our daily behaviors without drama.

I like you a lot

When you tell someone else "I like you" or "you make me happy," you're talking about your experiences and perceptions. This kind of expressions don't have so much to do with the other person, but with you.

The same happens when your significant other doesn't give you what you think you need. "You're unfair, selfish, I can't stand you." But, what does this have to do with the other person? It doesn't have anything to do with their traits, but with your expectations, perception, and feelings.

You're the only one responsible
for maintaining your peace, or losing it.

When your partner tells you something, although you're the message receiver, they're still the owner, and that's why the message will depend on how the issuer feels, but the effect on you will be the product of your own feelings and beliefs.

The clearer you are regarding your thoughts and feelings, the more you realize that the other people are responsible for what they say, as you are responsible for what you say.

Here's the place where peace can help you have good relationships with the people surrounding you, and this will help you cultivate more successful relationships.

When you reduce your reaction regarding
what others think of you,
you get to live with harmony.

When you realize that what they say belongs to them and they are just projecting that on you, you'll be able to stop reacting about and defending against what others think or say. When your partner tells you "I need you to change so I can be happy," it's pretty obvious she's lost in the nightmare of her thoughts. In the end, it's her business, and realizing this gives you freedom.

Let them be

No one can understand you fully and you can't understand the other people fully either. What we can do is connect with them, and this implies letting them be, understanding that sharing time and getting along making our lives as wonderful as possible.

We're the only ones who have to know ourselves, in the deepest way. So, in this way, we'll generate a relationship filled with joy and peace, and we'll be able to share it with other people.

Real understanding consists in recognizing that everything depends on how we see our reality. It can push us away or get us close to an authentic relationship. If we recognize that we can't form relationships in peace because we are in a continuous war with everything we do, say, and discover, we could warn our significant other that he or she would need to fight a battle to be able to connect with us.

When there's no self-esteem or appreciation towards ourselves, it's very hard to have healthy and peaceful relationship. We should drive our acts in order to live with balance and well-being within ourselves, so we can have strong foundations and recognize our value.

When we have inner peace, we become kind human beings, we automatically feel we love the other people, not as a consequence, but like something natural that emerges from us, away from intellectual movies.

*An undressed relationship means
giving yourself to the other people with freedom.*

Every moment is filled with you and me, beyond thoughts, ideas, and tags. If we live with ideas like "I need a relationship," or "I should make finding a relationship my life's purpose," we're going to suffer.

The truth is that our relationship won't be undressed if it is intellectual—that is to say, if we see other people as concepts, tags, roles, and the memories of past relationships, we'll be living in intellectual conditions of what our life and relationships should be.

The real thing is the present with determined people, experiences, and connections. Relationships are created at every turn and the way we form relationships has to do with our ability to give ourselves to life. This is only made within emptiness, out of expectations, although you may feel threatened or unprotected.

The source of nourishing relationships

H ave you asked yourself, where's the source of relationships, the thing that make them flourish and improve the reality of those who are involved?

There are many answers to this question, but the main thing is to realize that the one making this question is our brain, our rational part that doesn't read the subtle world of what can't be touched, seen, or heard. There are three dimensions in this world, and in relationships as well.

First-dimension relationships

These relationships are developed in an intellectual, theoretical, ideal, and imaginary sphere and the ones that live in one have a clear idea of what a good relationship is, but they are lost in ideas and definitions. Sometimes, they look for the impossible or pretend that everything is ideal and romantic.

Getting to know what a relationship is, looking at this reality and not the dictionary, won't make your expectations hurt you. The biggest suffering comes from the comparison your mind does between what it should be and the reality you have before you.

One must look at this reality and let their partner be free. He or she can choose anything, even when they don't agree with or can't adopt your preconceived ideas.

Second-dimension relationships

These ones are developed in two spheres, length and width (shape and content). It's concrete, it's materialized, it's not an ethereal idea, but a face, acts, and movements.

The relationship is nourished through gifts and time together. It grows, although you still don't share deeply what you both have inside, but you're still getting to know him or her.

It's important that the people involved in the relationship, when rushing in order to impress the other person or have a good time, must have fun and spend money according to their possibilities. That's how the relationship will continue in a healthy way, at every possible angle.

Life is simpler than it looks. What happens is that we complicate it when we want to be or look like something we are not. Then, you make high class gifts when you belong to a middle class, setting expectations that don't belong to your reality and, therefore, you won't be able to sustain for long.

If you complicate your life, you stop enjoying it. Someone that stops enjoying life stops growing up, and that's when you start looking for your development in any other place.

Third-dimension relationships

We can find something better and more nourishing in the third dimension, because this one adds an additional sphere in its development: the spiritual level.

Here's where energetic experiences are developed, with vitabytes, and they imply and provoke moods, emotions, feelings, and physical sensations. You get memories like foods, concerts, shows, sharing readings, commented photographs, handmade gifts, surprises, deep-breathing moments, funny moments, laughs, anecdotes that make you feel alive, transcendent events like childbirths or seeing special people go, happy and painful breakups, all sorts of communications, from a glance, a letter, a puppet...

It's fascinating to find out that this dimension is more nourishing and satisfying for the human being. You should do what you can in order to get filled with energy, because, in your relationships, what matters is your boost. You do things with it, and that amount of voltage (vitabytes) will generate an emotion. It´ll improve your mood, you voice tone will resonate and it'll shake everyone who hears you. The moment will become magic.

What you make someone feel becomes a unique experience, what you make someone feel is valuable and important.

You are what you provoke in the rest.

Remember you are a human being in process, you're always about to become someone able to relate harmoniously with yourself, with what's alive, with nature, life, the other people, and God.

The life purpose of all human beings is to connect with the kindness in those relationships and receive all of their consequences. You start with yourself, having unconditional love from your Creator, and radiate that God's presence towards other people, with high energy levels, because it's about something real and present, not just an idea.

The spiritual dimension is the one that gives us the best food in our relationships. In this dimension, we form a relationship from the wisest and most valuable part we have: the spirit that has eternal life.

The most important thing
when forming a relationship with someone
is to connect with their spirit.

That's the purpose of this temporary experience. Through a body, we can establish a connection between two people, so both of them get enriched and they fill their energy mutually.

The question here is how to connect to someone else's spirit. The answer is by working on yourself so much so you can live in this third dimension, first turning on your spirit or **WISE BEING**.

You can't have a connection with someone if your spirit isn't activated. This is an essential condition. To activate it, there are no recipes. You should have self-awareness and a dialogue with that inner wisdom that allows you to dig into what your life's purpose is, your vocation, what talents you can develop, and once you find them, serve the other people with them.

It's up to everyone to attain consciousness about this world's subtle parts in order to transform and enrich this reality and their relationships. If I get to develop my talent, connecting with that spiritual energy that fills me with pleasure when I do what makes me feel passionate, I'll find meaning in what I do. This is what Malcolm Gladwell was based on in order to affirm that investing ten thousand hours doing something will make you an expert.

The meaning of life is energy and the more you consume, the more it fills you.

If you work on your talent a lot, you'll have way more energy to continue and you'll be able to achieve Gladwell's ten thousand hours with pleasure, because in the subtle world, things are simple. The secret remains in finding what you will receive that energy from.

You sometimes act with magical confidence and that, in fact, actually is magic. Magic is when believing in a Superior Power, allowing you to develop your talent with time, with patience and humbleness, letting you be helped by the people you got to cultivate undressed relationships with.

Empathy: vibrating with someone else

There's nothing that can't generate a feeling. We need to get our ability to get excited about events back, because that's the ingredient that connects and links us with the full reality: odors, flavors, clothing, weather, people, animals, things...

When you're aware of what reality puts before you and you receive it as it is, without comparing it to a mental list about what you expected, that's the moment you'll be able to connect with someone else.

A nourishing and undressed relationship is generated when you attend emotions, sensations, and feelings. That's the moment where the connection and relationship starts and not just when checking what happened and why it happened.

That type of conversations only creates empty relationships where people interchange information at an intellectual level, but none of them are actually there. I'll write up an example.

A young girl calls her father because she was robbed. If she had an empty relationship with her father, the conversation would be more or less like this:

— *"Daughter, what happened? Tell me where you were when it happened?"*
— *"At the park, Dad."*
— *"And, how was the guy that robbed you?"*
— *"I don't remember him well, Dad."*
— *"What did he rob?"*
— *"My bag. I had all of my money and my cellphone there, Dad."*
— *"Don't worry, we're going to find the robber. Did you already report the cellphone?"*
— *"Yes, Dad."*
— *"Very good, my daughter."*

This conversation comes from a dad in an empty relationship, because he tries to play his "correct" role. Nevertheless, when you assume your dad role in an undressed relationship, the conversation would be like this:

— "Daughter, I found out you were robbed and I'd like to know how you feel now, are you okay?"

— "I'm very shocked and scared, Dad."

— "It's not surprised, but now I want you to close your eyes and breathe deeply, and imagine I'm with you and I'm hugging you with love and protection."

— "Thank you, Dad."

— "In this moment, I'm going to be where you are, my daughter. I just want you to know you have my support for whatever you need, and I'll try to solve this problem. Try to get your confidence and peace back. I'm sure you'll be able to solve everything. Who are you with in this moment?"

— "I'm alone here, Dad, at the police station, reporting the robbery."

— "Are they treating you well?"

— "Yes, Dad, they're all very kind."

— "Tell me more, my daughter. Please, don't hung up until I arrive at the police station."

This father has a relationship connected from the spirit with his daughter and he doesn't act according to preconceived social roles. The situation can look similar, but the peace a father can offer when he's connected with his daughter, is very high. It can support his daughter's decisions.

This type of support always strengthens us and gives us the ability to move on. Every experience is a lesson and one must live it through that connection. Everything that happens to you must be visualized as an opportunity to connect with others and create real bonds and relationships.

Always talking about unity and connecting is the key in this life. This connecting from the spirit produces the peace that gives us mental clarity, physical health, and emotional balance.

Relationships with things

Plenty of the things that surround you don't have life, but they are a part of your life. For example, if things could speak, what would they say about the treatment you give them? Do you spend your life offending them when they don't work? Or, perhaps, in your mess, you can't find them and then you curse them?

The usage you give them makes them work better or last longer. Being aware of how your relationship with things is can be good, because they are a part of the relationships that define you as a person.

I remember that a girl asked her father to look at how her boyfriend treated the car she was in, what its condition was, if it was clean, if it was organized and worked well, because that treatment would be extended to other relationships and it would surely be a sign of how he would treat her.

Imagine for a moment a surgeon who had all of his tools dirty and messed up in his operating room. Would you ask him to perform an open-heart surgery on your mother-in-law, assuming you want her to survive? If your mechanic had a disaster at his workshop, with old and broken tools and oils, would you be okay if he told you "don't worry, I know where things are in my mess"?

People that see
the way we form relationships with things,
trust us or decide not to trust us.

You can see people with dirty phones, with broken screens. Imagine, if they treat their phone like that, knowing they need to use it all day long, how would they treat you if they only stayed with you for a part of their time?

This type of observation gives us evidence about what we can expect from the people we have around us. It can also give us information about the treatment we offer to other people.

Your relationship with money

It's fundamental in this modern world to be aware of the way we use money, which is something apparently dead, it's simply paper. Many people have qualities in their lives, but their relationship with money is not taken care of and it's filled with wounds that make the little money they have disappear and the money they don't have, they already owe.

I'll talk about the essence of the relationship with money. This subject could be a whole book, but they're a lot of people that have already explained this subject. I'll just focus on essential points that aren't mentioned in other books about how to be rich.

Money is not paper,
although this is the vessel
we use to interchange it.

I invite you to take a dollar and read it. It clearly says what money is: trust.

When you give a hundred-dollar bill to someone for a product or service, what you're doing is telling them "I trust your product or service will actually cost a hundred dollars." In this way, my decision about going back with another hundred-dollar bill would be made. This type of trust is key, because it's what creates a link between money and other people.

First, in order to build your relationship with trust, it all starts with you and the money. A person that doesn't trust themselves can't trust other people. When you feel confident about generating money, you know you can spend it with confidence, because you are certain you can generate it again.

This freedom when spending money stops the pain. When someone feels that they're becoming poor when spending money, that's because they don't trust they can generate that amount of money again. This relationship with money is harmful and it'll make you poor.

I invite you to improve your relationship with money. Imagine, for a second, that money is a human being, someone that's next to you. Try to put a face to it, a name, a body. It's important to learn to get along with kindness.

When you talk about money, don't insult it, don't underestimate it, don't idealize it, don't demonize it, don't curse it. Bless it.

If money was a person, it wouldn't stay with someone that's cursing it, with someone talking bad about it. Instead, it would stay with someone that talks well about it, that uses it well, that understands how to thank it for everything it offers, and it would call this person its friend.

A good relationship with money is essential in having even more money. Another thing about money is that when you're greedy, you give it absolute power, but this isn't good either and it'll leave.

Imagine having someone near you that wants to control you all day long. They ask you what you did, where you went, what you thought, what you pretended, what plans you have... You'll end up asphyxiated and, surely, you'll leave.

*Having a balanced relationship with money
is fundamental in order for it to stay with you.*

Money allows you to live life experiences, it allows you to learn things, travel, build companies, give jobs, create products, and show how much you appreciate the people surrounding you. That's what money was made for.

You can't criticize money and say you don't like it because you have wrong ideas about it. Plenty of times, those ideas aren't even yours. You must learn to discover it. For Catholics, it's important to not accumulate wealth. In Protestantism, money is a blessing and a sign of predestination, so, the more you have, the closer you'll be to Heaven. Jews educate their children about the importance of money since the very beginning.

Money doesn't have a religious meaning, but a practical one. We live under a capitalist system. We gain money with honest work and we spend it in what we think adds value to our reality and our loved ones' reality.

This way, if your relationship with money will always be healthy and undressed, it'll stay in your house and leave whenever it has to leave. This means trust. If we gave it the appropriate treatment, money would come back, and it would come back with its friends: more money, opportunities, wealth, easiness to go further, safety, and trust.

When we do excellent work,
we deserve excellent payment.

Life loves excellence, which is giving more than what is expected from you. It's voluntarily giving more. It's to show the other people, with actions, that they're special.

For some reason, life loves excellence, and when we practice it, it gives us plenty of things, and among them is more money. This is the deep meaning behind the tip we pay in the restaurant when we are attended to incredibly well.

Life wants us to understand that it doesn't work by a necessity, it works by deservedness. When nature allows a seed to flourish, it's because it's strong and it deserves it. When we deserve the things we obtain, then we are in the successful and developed reality that grows.

Our wealth isn't abuse, but deservedness. No one gave us anything, we earned it with our behavior, discipline, desire to move forward and continue achieving what it seemed impossible to achieve.

Things don't arrive by themselves just because you need them, you pay the cost to life, which is the commitment and discipline to deserve them. When you find them through this path, you have the certainty and trust you can do it again, because you've already done it. This generates a healthy relationship with money.

Chapter 4

Relationship with the Eternal

An essential relationship for human beings is the relationship with the Eternal, which transcends death. This dimension affects the way you conceive and act in this temporary life and it's pretty common among all spiritual beings.

The human being that dies loses their aura and loses twenty-one grams; after that, eternity comes. The relationship with the eternal must be healthy, serene, and very real. It's not about having an intellectual relationship with eternity, it's about living and experiencing it while going through a life that doesn't stop.

I hear plenty of people saying they don't believe in this eternity and, nevertheless, in their hardest moments, they pray. The human spirit shows up and makes you recognize a Superior Power. There are plenty of moments in your life where you are surrounded by miracles, magic, and the divinity that don't have an earthly explanation. I want you to go back to these experiences. In this relationship with the eternal, you can make anything you live through be meaningful and find the spiritual mission you came to complete in this temporary life.

*A life without a spiritual
meaning is frustrating and difficult to endure.*

Facing an insufferable pain, we may become insane or commit suicide. Instead, a healthy relationship with the eternity leads us to a wonderful, magic, spectacular, and miraculous path.

Inner wisdom

The relationship with the Eternal covers the relationship with your life's purpose, the transcendental part, Logos (word), and your **WISE BEING**.

The words we pronounce talk about our life's purpose, our inner being, and the most valuable thing, the Eternal. That's why the word has such a strength that it affects the reality you're creating.

*What you say and the emotions you
do it with modify your reality.*

We aren't just a body. We make our reality more comfortable or unpleasant with our words. We can transform words into a touch or a punch.

Being aware of how we talk to ourselves and the people that surround us creates a superior level of consciousness. Also, the dialogue with the Spirit helps us find new ways. This way, we can unveil our life's mission, one step at a time.

Our **WISE BEING** is the most valuable part we have, but in our comings and goings, we don't take care of it, so we don't know how to interpret it.

This inner voice filled with wisdom talks to you through this reality. When this reality asks you for something, dare to do crazy things. Reality talks through what happens to us, the people we have around us, our feelings, illnesses, accidents, miracles, opportunities, relationships, our sense of humor, our breathing. The problem is that we don't receive the message, so we stay ignorant.

God talks to us bluntly
through the inner and outer reality.

I can assure you that this reality screams. The problem is that we don't hear it, because of our ego that forces us to hear only what our mind says.

Remember that our mind talks at a level that's not necessarily real. It tends to deny what reality and God tells us, that's why it's so harmful and arrogant. It was Adam's and Eve's minds that made them stop hearing God.

They let themselves get tricked, because the preferred to hear the father of lies.

Many people in the current era talk about the mind's power and they elevate it to God. It's an exaggeration that people buy and approve. The truth is that when looking at the lives of those preachers that claim we should focus on thinking what we create, we find that none of it is true.

Our mind was designed to measure, not to plan, nor to launch anything. When you live listening to the creator of Life, reality smiles at you, as well as the results walking with you.

When there's no successful results in your life, you should ask yourself when you got distracted and started to listen to your mind, instead of connecting to your inner part and an observation without prejudices regarding the outward reality.

There are gurus that offer you the stars, but will they actually take you to them?

The real winner is the one that experiences and gives a meaning to everything happening around them, taking the best of it to improve this reality and the people surrounding them. This is done in the dimension of the Spirit.

The human spirit is made for big things. Don't allow your **MIND THAT LIES** or your mediocre self, drive your existence and make out of it just an attempt to survive or a quest for immediate satisfaction that doesn't last, which makes us dependent on something that controls us.

Everything you do towards life gives you energy, your soul gets undressed, and it takes you to find another human being that also dares to be undressed.

I don't "believe" in God because I know Him, because I live hearing Him and letting Him speak through me. I read it in this reality surrounding me. I find Him every time I find things I struggle to accept. Things are lived, not rationalized.

Life is lived and not analyzed.

Cultivate your intuition

The spirit is able to guess, to get to know, without any sort of mental arguments.

It's inclined to a communion, understood as the ability to communicate with God through logos, the inner wisdom and consciousness. This latter allows us to correct and improve the patterns the divine expresses when hearing its voices.

Cultivate your undressed
relationship with the Eternal,
enjoy your life's experience and share it.

Growing up with someone else

Take into consideration that this spiritual path doesn't have to be explored alone. Life moves all the time, it's conjugated as a gerund and the gerund gets to have the best company. Many forces are better than one.

When enhancing your spiritual side, make sure your partner is growing with you as well, because when you grow a lot and your partner doesn't, your interests change, the relationship gets weaker. If you don't receive what you need, you'll be tempted to look for it in someone else.

Some of the couples that come to me realize they're far away from their partner. One of them is in a higher level, while the other one remains at the wild, comfortable state. The relationship will disappear if they don't do something extreme.

Life: an adventure and a game

This life is an adventure and at the same time, a test, or maybe, a game. We require all of these elements in our relationships in order to become winners, to become whole and fulfilled people.

Let's remember that we're wild beings and we need the eternal spirit to display our dignity.

We need a **WISE BEING** that overcomes the **MIND THAT LIES** and transforms what happens to us and what we do into a life purpose that satisfies us.

This is the something that's worth creating for you and your loved ones.

The meaning you give your life
keeps you alive.

In his book "*Man's Search for Meaning*," Viktor Frankl says that in concentration camps, he found that people waking up without a purpose would die in less than two weeks, whereas people with a sick mother, a child with down syndrome, a wife waiting for them, or projects to start, would find the way to survive against the hardships.

I believe that they were fed by their positive info-energy, so they were pushed to react towards the exterior adversity with creativity.

Anyone that has "what to I live for,"
will find "how" to do it.

When I ask my students if they want a relationship and their answers is affirmative, I tell them to connect with their info-energy to find a way out. Only then do they start to have clear ideas. This is the best practice.

What meaning have I given to my life?

It's not about a theoretical meaning, but knowing what I have been following. Life is a gerund, it's not a theory, nor is it stable, and it doesn't stop, it's a movement and it goes towards a destiny. That destiny is your purpose in life. Discover and be aware of the meaning or purpose you've chosen, perhaps unconsciously, by the decisions you have made up to today. Life is a mystery and I'd be lying to you if I told you I knew exactly what this life's meaning was, although we can find the key in relationships. The lives of each individual go towards a place and that place must be something valuable for you and consciously sought after as a goal, so that when you arrive, you'll know you've accomplished your mission.

The worst thing that could happen to you is wanting to go to the north and finding out you've been walking to the south.

Finding a purpose in life or finding out which destination you've been going towards is very important, it's about a place you want to go and, mostly, who you want to become at the end of your life.

Not only is it a goal or an objective, but also the reason you now decide everything you decide.

Committed to peace

A long time ago I decided to commit to the time relativity and that no matter what happened to me, I'd try to look for peace.

Before every situation, I stop, observe, and work on what I need to do to get peace, although sometimes I have to modify my reaction, because I find myself not having peace. Then I return to my path, because I am committed to remaining in a deep and inner state of peace.

My invitation is for you to discover your purpose and choose to embrace it or change it consciously. See what works for you; what doesn't work and pushes you away from your purpose, let it go. Choose what your purpose in life is, and get attached to it as a huge tool for clarity, as the compass that enlightens your path.

Discover your mission

It's never too late to discover your mission in life, and this is deeper than the activity you dedicate your time to or what you've studied. Just dive in and search deep in your soul, as well as in the signs and "coincidences" of reality that guide you to a destination. Adolescence and our life's second half are good moments to bring this mission up.

*No one escapes from their mission
and those are the good news.*

Jean Monbourquette says that someone can change their job without modifying their personal mission whatsoever. "If we compare accomplishing a mission with a musical piece execution, the mission would be the melody, whereas the job, the function, or career, would be the instruments."

The purpose in life isn't in books, Monbourquette adds, because some people look in philosophy and theology for a clue to identify their purpose. There's no doubt that such approaches can be useful to define a purpose in life, but they aren't *the* purpose. To find it, the formula is clear:

Know yourself.

Sometimes, people confuse their "talents" with their traits. A talent is a coin, it's the wealth the Creator put in you. Although He may have given you a huge talent for singing, you're not forced to dedicate yourself to it. It doesn't matter if society insists and makes you feel you've wasted your potential, the purpose in life is not about having potential, but what you heart tells you. Once I knew a girl that always won piano contests, however, although she loved playing the piano, she didn't want to dedicate her life to it, because she felt being an educator was her calling.

The social pressure was so big, because of her "**incredible talent**" that she dedicated to playing piano professionally, but she didn't feel fulfilled. It wasn't until she started staying with terminal patients that she felt for the first time she followed her heart.

The important thing is that when looking for your mission, you have to learn to let the past go.

"What the caterpillar calls the end of the world, the master calls a butterfly"
—Richard Bach

In this metamorphosis that implies getting rid of the past, it is very important for you to know your true identity, so you can get rid of superficial tags.

Ask yourself: "Who am I?" Perhaps you'll answer things related to your job, your studies, social status, nationality, character traits, your familiar and social function, but you have to go deeper to get rid of these superficial tags.

I propose an exercise for you, devised by Monbourquette himself, that will help you decipher this answer.

Write at the very center of a piece of paper your name inside a circle. Over the next ten minutes ask yourself, "Who am I?" and write the words that come to you. When you're finished, classify every single word.

- **First category**: Everything related to your job, function, social status, nationality, studies, afiliation. For example, Pedro, Mexican engineer, teacher, father, Enrique's son.
- **Second category**: Positive and negative traits, like shy, extroverted, happy, dreamer, friendly, affectionate, organized, angry.
- **Third category**: Spiritual ideals that go beyond your job, essentially what one has in the heart. For example, collaborator, healer, selfless.
- **Fourth category**: This is the hardest ones, because it refers to the person's identity. Few words can fit in here. Perhaps words like, me, my name, and human being.

Now, change the verb **to be** to the verb **to have**, and apply it to each one of these categories, but use the verb **to be** only in the fourth category. So you "have a career," you "have a teacher's role," you "have a bond with your father Enrique," you "have the habit of being organized," you "have the virtue of friendship," you "have a healer's mission," but "you are a man," "I am me, I am a human being, I am <name>."

There are plenty of disidentification exercises that can help you feel lighter, without the burden of so many roles, so you can get closer to your center, your deepest identity, your essence.

Start your path towards discovery and apply what you find in your life!

Lourdes' trip

Her life had to be something more than that endless succession of meaningless days and, in order to discover the meaning of her life, she had to let some masks fall off, one by one...

Remembering...

Our protagonist, Lourdes Vargas, had never found any meaning in her marriage and life, except for her brilliant children Gustavo and Aldo.

Married since a very young age with the prestigious Dr. Humberto Elizalde, Lourdes spent her time doing futile activities, because it was a habit among high society ladies.

Always locked up in herself, Martha Zaida, her loyal club friend, hadn't even trespassed her fence of disdain and arrogance.

One afternoon, her husband had an awful car accident and he ended up injured, as well as his companion, a mysterious woman called Ana Claudia who Lourdes didn't know and, according to the medical report, the woman lost the two-month twins she had been carrying inside her.

The way events elapsed revealed to Lourdes and her family a truth they didn't suspect, that allowed her to see many more aspects of her life and herself that she didn't know.

Resentful and angry, she decided that silence was the best revenge, so she started holding on to her pain, anger, and suffering, until an emotional collapse stopped her.

Then, she lived a new experience that allowed her to have a meeting with herself in another dimension. There, her **WISE BEING***, gave her all of the information she needed in order to go back to her world and restore her relationships...*

The story goes on like this...

Lourdes tried to open her eyes, but her vision was blurry. At a distance, she heard the peculiar electrocardiograph sound with her heartbeats. She suddenly heard altered voices she couldn't distinguish.

Little by little, she started to regain her consciousness and clarity of mind, and started to feel her body again. Her lips were dry, and she felt her muscles were waking up, one by one.

The sounds were clearer. She recognized her son's, Aldo's voice, who called Gustavo and rang a sort of bell that was alarming. She felt her son's hand on her face.

He told her, "Mom, can you hear me?"

She thought she was still in that Paradise, but she wasn't feeling her body like she had been feeling it before.

Now, it was heavy and dense, as it had always been. She opened her eyes and saw her son's worried face, calling her with tears about to burst out.

She wanted to answer, but she couldn't even move her neck. She wanted to talk, but the words stayed in her mind. There was no sound in her throat.

She saw doctors and nurses come, but she didn't understand what was happening. There were a lot of people and the noise bothered her. Every hand that touched her felt like an act of aggression.

She felt helpless, although she knew they were doing something good for her. She slowly realized that she was in a hospital room.

She didn't know how nor when she arrived there. She wanted to remember, but her brain was still half awake.

Again, she heard, "Mom!"

This time it was her other son, Gustavo, and that was an energy boost for her memory. She remembered having gone to the chapel crying after her children proposed to Humberto, their father, to go teach at the university in a wheelchair.

She also remembered how much she cried, and her childhood memories. That's how she arrived at the magical meeting she had had with herself and Rita. Then, she got worried, she was scared that she had forgotten every word and lesson. However, she thought over the meeting and everything was there, safe and fresh, as if everything had happened a few seconds ago.

That made her laugh, but her muscles hadn't moved for a long time, so she felt her face barely creak.

When she finally opened her eyes, she recognized her two children behind a man that was familiar and yet also strange. His features were unmistakable, but he had an expression she'd never seen before. He was sitting in a wheelchair near her bed, skinnier, grayer than what she remembered.

She needed a few seconds to recognize him, she had to mentally scan every part of his skin, every gesture pronouncing her name. It was like she was redesigning that man that, to be honest, she had never seen thoroughly before, despite having spent almost thirty years as his wife.

The only thing that seemed to be there, untouched, immaculate, was that deep brightness in his eyes that she had seen the first time they had been in bed together. As incredible as it could seem, Lourdes had the same sensation she had that day. They looked at each other in such a way that everyone around them remained silent before that magical connection that suddenly filled the hospital room.

In that moment, Lourdes and Humberto met again for the first time. The moment was interrupted by the doctor, her children's friend, who got close to bed to tell her:

— "Good morning, Lourdes, can you talk?"

Lourdes nodded little by little and her throat got clearer.

— "Yes," *she answered imperceptibly.*

Her children hugged her while Humberto didn't release her hand. Inexplicably, that heat relived her little by little. She felt she was someone different and also that everyone else had changed. She could see it.

The doctor explained the numbers from the tests, he said he was still waiting on some results but he would get them soon, because they were very important.

Lourdes stopped paying attention to him. She didn't listen to him anymore, she was just focused on enjoying everything she was feeling.

Two days passed during which, every time Lourdes opened her eyes, she saw Humberto with her and, sometimes, her children as well. Even the hospital food was good, and she felt gratitude that was new and strange for her, as though it came from a place within her she hadn't found yet.

Humberto looked tired. She would wake up at night to see him with a light blanket on the sofa. She felt tenderness for him and even though they were never awake at the same time, she had the certainty that the same happened to him when he looked at her sleeping.

She thought about them a lot, about their life together, the years she didn't focus on him, this idea about fulfilling social rules just because they were married, the reason she didn't focus on being present in the relationship.

They both became another object in the house and, somehow, she felt Humberto had the same thoughts.

When she had gathered enough strength, she finally left the hospital. Her children went with her when she was discharged and, when going out, the scene was kind of like a frame from those movies you can no longer forget: each one of her children carried a wheelchair bearing one of their parents, because, although Lourdes could walk, those were the hospital's rules. While they were moving forward, Humberto took her hand softly. Their children looked at each other with uncertainty and hope, but smiling.

When they went home, everything seemed wonderful. Every single thing was exactly like she remembered it, but, at the same time, she felt everything smiling at her. She remembered one of the lessons she received in her deep dream.

Life gives you what you give it.

It was around seven o'clock and her children took her to her room. They gave her a kiss and said to her and their father goodbye, but they asked before if they needed something else. Lourdes and Humberto said no, they knew they were close to a moment where they needed to have a mandatory talk no one could avoid.

During those days, Humberto was more used to his wheelchair and he even seemed like an expert. She noticed it when he was going to the closet, but she didn't say anything, because she didn't know how he would interpret it. It was strange to discover that she didn't know him deeply, despite the years.

He opened a drawer, put something on his lap, and turned around. She couldn't avoid crying when she saw it was her pajamas. He started to cry too. He approached her and when they were face to face, they hugged. None of them knew what was happening to them.

It was like they gave in to each other during the hug, like they were making love with their souls, as if they knew their goal now was to seize the time they had together, because they had already wasted a lot of it.

In a few seconds, both went through hard life lessons in which they could have been separated. If they did separate, it was because they still had to learn something important.

When they stopped the hug, something made them feel united. The talk they had needed since years ago was silent.

There were almost no words.

Almost whispering, he said, "I love you."

Lourdes looked at him for a few seconds. Although she knew the words, she didn't know how to pronounce them, but she noticed in Humberto's eyes that he wasn't expecting an answer. There was no accusation in his eyes.

Slowly, he started to help her dress in her pajamas. Lourdes felt she ran out of air when those hands touched her skin, her heart speeded up and, at the same time, the room's silence allowed his heart to be heard, until the two sounds was just one. Without a doubt, they were making love.

They looked at each other, beyond their eyes. Lourdes felt the boost to undo his shirt. She needed to feel him and she didn't care about anything, not even the difficulty he'd have about moving without a leg.

They were about to find something that had been near to them during their whole life and they never noticed. She felt every millimeter of his skin, something that took her, as though a stream of water, towards Humberto's kisses. When touching and finding him, she felt she was finding herself. For the first time, she was experimenting passion.

When she started to analyze why she felt that way, then she realized she didn't need to think of anything. What was that that was so hers, that made her feel in her field, that was a part of her and went beyond her body, as a fusion no one could separate? Was that love?

She closed his eyes and got close to his face. She breathed his air and, without touching his lips, they were already kissing. Their senses were more awake than ever, they felt every touch deep into their souls. He grabbed her face and felt the humidity of a tear. He wasn't surprised, but, with his finger, he touched it and it felt like happiness and fulfillment.

They'd never forget that instant. When their lips touched, they felt electricity, their breathing grew harder, until they got to be finally naked, not their body, but their soul. They knew that, after that night, there was nothing else to discover. They saw their most sublime side.

The moment they were building was something more than physical. None of them remembered that he was missing a leg nor that she was missing a heart. They complemented each other according to their deficiencies.

He felt he didn't miss anything, and he wouldn't feel like this with anyone else. He would never get undressed without anyone else, and much less make love without feeling affected because of the limb he lacked.

She felt something was beating in her chest and didn't know if it was her heart or Humberto's heart. In any case, it didn't matter anymore, because hearts were beating at the same rhythm. They were building a relationship in the fourth dimension.

There's no need to narrate what happened afterwards. Let's leave in the intimacy of that room the details of that magical night.

They hugged the whole night, they didn't understand how they survived so many years without loving each other. It seemed unthinkable now. Their laughter in the middle of darkness revealed the serenity that total self-giving can give you.

The first sunbeam surprised them, they had never appreciated how beautiful the morning was from their bedroom.

They were hugging, skin to skin and, without knowing, they thought the same: they wished that that moment would never end, and they immortalized it in a whisper. They knew that at that point they only had each other and they didn't regret it at all.

He hugged her hard and she shuddered again, the dream was just a pause for their new love and they continued enjoying the fact they finally knew each other.

That day everything started again, like a second chance. They woke up and, for the first time, they took a shower together, despite Humberto needing extra help.

Without thinking, Lourdes helped him enter the bathtub, and she entered as well. There wasn't much to say, sensuality was in the air.

The housekeeper got surprised when Lourdes said she would prepare breakfast herself and she got even more surprised when she saw Humberto with a smile she'd never seen before.

The housekeeper didn't know what to do, but there was no doubt that something strange had happened. She even thought that maybe they had won the lottery and, somehow, she was right. They had finally undressed their relationship and they looked exactly like they were, without disguises nor masks.

While Lourdes cooked, Humberto observed and admired her. He guessed at the curves under her apron that made him love her decades ago. She discovered him looking at her and she blushed with an ashamed and teenage-like smile and he saw those dimples beside her mouth he loved so much again and hadn't seen since a long time ago, to the point he had forgotten them.

Lourdes served the breakfast with delicacy. The coffee's smell gave a new meaning to the house. It smelled like they were newlyweds, when everything was an illusion and a discovery.

They laughed a lot when tasting the breakfast and noticed it didn't have salt, they laughed like they forgave everything, and make it a reason to be an unforgettable moment, another story for the album of memories.

They finished their breakfast and looked at each other expecting what the following thing was. Their life was now a blank book expecting to be filled, excited and anxious, with new stories.

Humberto asked her:

— "Do you remember the last time we walked together?"
— "No, I don't remember," Lourdes answered.
— *He continued,* "Would you like to go to the park with me?"
— "The park? Of course! I'm going to let the kids know."
— "Don't do it, Lourdes, it's not necessary."
— "But, what if"

Humberto interrupted her lovingly:

— "What if, what? Nothing's going to happen, my love. At the beginning it was just you and me, do you remember? We got lost little by little in the role of parents.
We forgot about us. We only enjoyed one year, then Gustave arrived and, from that moment, our roles as spouses started to fade away.
Don't you think it's time to start again? It's never too late, now it's just you and me again."

Lourdes reflected for a few seconds. Humberto's words were deep and wise, but she was stuck on that "my love" that resonated like music in her heart.

She got close to her husband and hugged him as though she hugged a lifesaver, whispering, "Let's go."

She helped him get in the car and on the way to the parl, she reflected about all of the hardships her husband had to face in order to do daily things.

She realized she'd been absent during Humberto's process and she felt guilty when she thought that he'd surely suffered a lot during that time, without counting the violent episode with the slap in the bedroom months ago.

It was inevitable to compare her aggressive behavior towards Humberto to his behavior when she was at the hospital, always so elegant and adorable with her.

Then, her **MIND THAT LIES** *seized the mood and her memories, and put her on a trap:*

— "Lourdes, remember, he cheated on you. Yes! That one, the woman with him in the car that was pregnant, she'd have had twins and she also cheated on her husband."

She felt that pain and had a regression. She became that selfish and destroying being again that she was before the celestial revelation, and she felt again like that implacable woman she'd been during her whole life.

She felt that familiar bitterness in her cells again and clutched the steering wheel resentfully. She was so confused. She didn't know if it was stupid to talk about the subject now when she was living something she had never imagined... What if she ruined everything again?

Nevertheless, the damage was done. Although it didn't last more than few seconds, that thought made her feel desperate and she wasn't going to pretend to be calm for long.

In the meantime, Humberto was happy, looking through the window at the path filled with trees, feeling the morning's fresh air on his face, because he hadn't do so for a long time. He was even whistling, following a melody on the radio.

That's why he was so shocked and bewildered when Lourdes stopped the car abruptly, the tires squeaking, turning the steering wheel towards the side of the road.

Humberto shook strongly and his instinct was to extend his arms to hold onto anything he could.

He was breathing hard and was trembling, and his surprise didn't let him speak, but, when he looked at Lourdes for an explanation, he found her looking in front of her, at the path, without moving.

After a few seconds, the conversation was like this:

— "Lourdes! What happens? You almost killed me! Why did you stop in such a way? Are you crazy?"
— "I had to do it, it was an impulse."
— "An impulse? Of what? Trying to kill me?"

Then, she turned her face to look at him.

— "Something like that," she answered.

— "Let's see, Lourdes, what are you talking about? A couple of minutes ago you were the perfect wife, and now you want to kill me?"

— "Oh, yes? I was the perfect wife? Wouldn't that be because I erased from my memory everything that happened?"

Humberto noticed that bitterness he knew pretty well in her sarcastic tone and saw how his wife turned into a cold and arrogant woman incapable of showing love again. He couldn't avoid thinking out loud.

— "I knew it, it was too good to be true. The honeymoon didn't last much, just a few hours."

That was a low punch for Lourdes, because at heart, she knew she should have thought things through. Nevertheless, her pride told her she had done well. Her inner fight was so intense that she wished to disappear. She wished the earth would swallow her up, in that moment, because she didn't have any idea about what to do and frustration was drowning her. That's what the **MIND THAT LIES** *does.*

She closed her eyes trying to escape, then she felt as though someone was rewinding her movie. In that moment, she had a regression and she faced again her angelical self. In a few seconds, she could revise each one of the words that were interchanged in that meeting with the **WISE BEING.**

— "Remember Lourdes, it's not the person you have to take care of, but the relationship, because it changes and moves all the time. Unconditional love isn't love, it's an undressed relationship, loving without expecting if the other person fills you or not. You offer a relationship that you give yourself. "When I look at someone else, the origin is my thought about them. Therefore, that idea is mine.

The **other** person doesn't exist. The **other people** don't exist. Human beings manipulate one another, they're not aware that they beg for happiness and that's why that feeling of effort exists. They're the only species in this planet that gets tired of living and require the society and the other members of the species to make them happy.

That's blackmailing. Every relationship has a goal, feeling total acceptance from you and what's really happening. Cohabitation is, before anything else, sharing. Participating in the lives of the other people and make them participate in our own life. The purpose of life is to grow and share.

No relationship is forever, just the relationship you have with yourself. Mammals aren't designed for monogamy and the human being is a mammal. Human nature requires stability, but not monogamy, that's been confused. The undressed relationship comes when you're ready and it goes when it's not real and, if it belongs to you, it'll return.

There are no big problems, but small people, and there are not bad relationships, but sick people in them. When you appreciate what you have, you have everything you need. Lourdes, not everything you see and believe is real..."

These words came to her in a second. She realized that her **WISE BEING** *revealed what happened to her clearly in that moment, but she was letting herself be dominated by the* **MIND THAT LIES.** *Then, she thought:*

— "I have the information, but, mostly, I have the decision to use this moment to grow, defeating my mind. I have the possibility in my hands to finally create an undressed relationship, or to continue on the bitter path of self-betrayal, and I know that that's not what I wish for my life."

Then, she returned to the present, and looking at her husband, she pronounced the words Humbert would have never thought he would hear from her lips.

— "I'm sorry, please forgive me."
— He doubted that he heard right.
— "What did you say?"
— "I said I am sorry, Humberto, really. I'm tired of living like this. My **Wise Being** just reminded me that if I want to be happy in the time I stay with you, I have to undress my soul and say everything I've got to say that has poisoned my life until now. I can't do it anymore, it drowns me."

Humberto didn't understand anything Lourdes just said, but, although he was scared, he got also hopeful. She continued:

— "I don't know where to begin nor how to tell you this, but when I was in the hospital, I had an encounter with myself, with my wise side.

It helped me understand that I have committed mistakes when I tried to carry this fake marriage, this fake commitment. I was actually never in love with you. I didn't marry you feeling this wild craziness that one's supposed to feel, nor that peace that you feel when you're with the right person.

I only felt the commitment our families had, and I know that, one way another, we were game pieces. Nevertheless, if we had known how to build a relationship, no matter how we got there, we would surely have done it well. We aren't the ones to blame, because we really didn't know how to do it.

That doesn't matter now. We only have 'today' and what we went through to get here. From now on, I wish to have a real relationship with you. We got married to satisfy this society, but we've never had an undressed relationship and, for that, one only needs to wish for it and work for it every moment to build it, like last night, when we did what we couldn't do after so many years. I want to tell you that last night I fell in love with you.

If you wish so, today I want to start a new life where we don't care about the other people, where we become our own priority, where no one gets to know us as much as we know ourselves, where we get to be happy during the rest of our lives."

While he listened to her, Humberto couldn't stop crying. He couldn't believe that he was finally hearing what he had expected throughout his whole life. When she stopped speaking, she looked at him and cried, too. They looked like kids that didn't know if they were crying because of pain or joy. There was no doubt that something magical had just happened.

They spent a long time enjoying that moment, so they looked at each other again. Lourdes had never seen her husband's feelings like that. It shook her to get to know that part of a man that she always thought of as "Dr. Elizalde," so comfortable in his role as if he was born playing it.

Humberto cleaned his face and took her hand. He said:

— "I don't know how to explain what I feel now. I've wished for this moment so much that now that happened I feel like I'm dreaming. I want to tell you something I've never told you...

I loved you from the very first day I saw you, in that family dinner, when we were just kids. I talked to my parents so you could be my wife and now that you tell me you were never in love with me, it breaks my heart to realize that I probably ruined your life... Forgive me, please! Those were different times, different habits, you know. Our parents supported those situations that, I now realize, were so wild. Marrying off a beautiful young girl with someone she hadn't even looked at, just because that man dreamed of her every night..."

This time it was Lourdes who couldn't believe what he was saying.

— "You're telling me that *you* asked your parents and they arranged everything with my parents, just because one day you thought of me being your wife?"

Humberto nodded without speaking. Thinking that that could be the end of everything created a lump in his throat. He didn't want to wake up from that dream that had lasted just one minute, one he had been waiting for his whole life. Finally, he gathered the necessary courage to say:

— "Since the first day I saw you, I knew I wanted to be with you forever."

There was a silence that seemed endless, until Lourdes answered

— "And why did you never tell me? Why didn't you do anything to show that?"

— "My father had a talk with me. He told me that he'd support me, because it was important for his interests as well, but first he told me something I'll never forget. 'Son, never tell a woman how much you love her, because that's the moment you lose your control on your marriage.

A good portion of indifference makes her fall in love and always keeps her uncertain about infidelity. Then she'll make a bigger effort when attending you.'

These words remained in my mind for years. I didn't want to be indifferent with you, I wanted to hold you the whole day and kiss you every time I saw you... But I was afraid my dad was right and that one day you'd leave me side, without realizing that adorable, sweet and young lady I fell in love with was dying day after day because I followed a stupid man's advice.My father thought my mom had stayed with him until the end because of his indifference, but she actually did it because she didn't have any value. I'm sorry for it, my love, forgive me, please."

Without realizing, after so many years together, they were finally undressing their souls.

Lourdes felt a mixture of pain, love, and something like flattery, because she's been loved for so long. Nevertheless, she couldn't stop thinking what would have happened if Humberto's father knew how to love. Without a doubt, the speech would have been very different, as well as her life.

Humberto continued:

— "I made so many mistakes during these years, but I think the biggest one I made was getting used to live like this. Another one was always wanting to be the best at everything, a well-known doctor, looking for your admiration, but I was wrong. Now I understand that you need to touch a woman's soul so she can fall in love with you. That's when you make love... But I just found that out yesterday, Lourdes. You don't know how sorry I am.

I didn't have the courage to make love before, because every day I saw you pull further away, get harder, and more resentful. I was scared of getting close to you and, instead of facing it, I decided to continue like that, until I had the car crash and I realized that life could leave in just an instant. I felt so frustrated when I saw that when I could have given you the best of me, I didn't. I realized that when I lost my leg. My soul hurt, Lourdes, you have no idea how much it hurt, that day. When you got close to give me my medicine, it was worse, because you never had a gesture like that one and you had it exactly when I felt most frustrated.

I actually didn't raise my hand towards you. It was an involuntary act against the idea of receiving the proof of your love when I couldn't give you the best of me physically anymore. And then, when you slapped me, it was the end for me. Now I see that I deserved it, I deserved more than that, for having wasted a life towards you, towards my love."

Lourdes heard him carefully while drying both of their tears. It felt so good touching his skin that she didn't want to stop doing it.

— "I don't blame you, Humberto. No one taught us anything. Just like you, I followed my mother's example; a woman without aspirations, only seeking to survive. Nevertheless, if all of it worked in order to have this moment together, then I don't regret it.

Having our children was also a blessing. They kept us together. Without them, no one would have resisted the cold of our house. Now, as parents, we should give them an example of what an undressed relationship looks like, so they can have a different life and stop repeating the same patterns of behaviors."

Suddenly, Lourdes was in silence. When hearing her own words, she remembered Ana, the woman in the car crash, and wondered if it was a good moment to talk about it.

— "What are you thinking about?" *Humberto asked.*
— "I like a lot everything we're talking about... I'd like to ask a question, but I'm afraid I'll ruin everything."
— "But, if you don't ask me, how are we going to have that undressed relationship you talk about?" *he told her.*
— "Alright... At the day of your accident we arrived at the hospital and they gave us a report of your health. A nurse told me you were with a woman, and she was pregnant with twins. Her husband arrived a bit later than us and. He got a stroke when he knew his children died. We all assumed they were your children."

— "Lourdes... I'm going to tell you a story. Ana has been my coworker for a long time now. She's the head of the nursing staff at the hospital where I work, a very professional woman committed to her career.
Two months before the accident, she left the hospital very late and, when going home, she was intercepted on

her way to her car and was assaulted. Nevertheless, the robbers weren't happy with it, so they decided to kidnap her along with taking car.

She was sexually abused and abandoned in a remote place, where she was found the very next day, without clothes and very hurt in both her body and soul. The news was very hard for all of us at the hospital and several doctors and I were in charge of attending to her. She and her husband had been married for seven years and they still couldn't have babies, because he had health problems. He'd started a fertility treatment and, a few weeks after that, when she was still healing after the attack, the results arrived. She was pregnant with twins. It was a very shocking moment, because now they didn't know if the pregnancy was a result from the treatment or the abuse she suffered.

As you can imagine, that generated a very deep emotional imbalance and we all made sure she wasn't alone. She wanted to abort the babies, because, although they could be her husband's babies, she felt that, emotionally, she could no longer be a good mother.

Her husband was afraid she was going to do something insane. He did want the babies, no matter what their origin was. The day of the accident, I invited her to go with me to a surgery, because, although she wasn't ready to work, we tried to maintain her busy doing other things outside her situation. That was the reason she was with me."

Lourdes was mute. She could only think of that woman's suffering after everything she'd lived through, and her husband's suffering who was also going through a delicate and emotional situation that had even affected his health. Finally, when she could articulate words, she said:

— "Why did you never tell me?"
— "How could I, Lourdes, if our only conversations were the bills to pay, complaints, and judgment towards your club friends? Starting with a certain Martha Zaida. You always had something bad to say about her."

Lourdes reflected about it and realized it was true. Martha Zaida was her main conversation subject when criticizing. What if she was wrong about Martha, as well as she was about Ana? How many things does the mind create without knowing which one is true?

— "Everything that I have been thinking is incredible. I wonder if anything my mind created has anything to do with reality. Forgive me, Humberto, for everything I believed about you. I supposed Ana was your lover and she cheated on her husband with you."

After reflecting, Humberto answered:

— "I have something more to tell you. Ana's subject tormented me for months, because I was isolated and I felt responsible. I realized you supposed she was my lover, but I didn't say anything, because I wanted to wait to see if your reaction was at least filled with jealousy. I'm not going to say that during these years I didn't have adventures, because of that lack of tenderness and understanding between us. I apologize for it. I was a coward and, now, if you forgive me, I want to start again with you. I want to live the rest of my life making one woman happy: you."

They looked at each other without saying anything. There were no secrets, no webs. They blended in a hug that would last even if their physical bodies separated, because it was a soul hug.

From that moment, they started living an undressed and real love. They felt like teenagers with an adult's maturity and the excitement when getting each other surprised them like kids when finding something new. Some months passed and everything at home was different, even their children started to visit more frequently and with more enthusiasm than ever. During the weekends, they both came with their spouses, and one of them would make Lourdes and Humberto grandparents.

Although they had had just a little time since their new life had started, they were so connected that no one that met them would believe their story. One November, Humberto proposed to Lourdes again. It was the most magical and special night of her life. Her children were so surprised that they couldn't stop asking what happened to them. Of course they shared everything they went through, from the chauvinist grandfather's advice, Lourdes' angelical moment, up to that day and how they wanted to leave to their children a legacy of love and transparency, of total surrender and passion, of not hiding anything, just undressing the soul.

Everything happened like in a fairytale. Humberto was already teaching at the university for months now and he had learned to drive to the school without anyone's help. He was motivated and happy.

Lourdes returned to the club one afternoon and, although she wanted to look unnoticed, it was impossible. Her friends hugged her. They knew everything she had gone through during that absence. Those things are always known, although no one knows how.

The only person that was very dedicated to contacting her was Martha Zaida, exactly the one she avoided the most. The others that used to appreciate her a lot did send their best wishes and blessings, nevertheless, just once.

Martha Zaida never replied her, despite being the only one interested in being her friend. That day, she was the only one that gave her one of those hugs that the soul can feel, one of those from the heart, and her eyes got a bit teary when she saw her. Lourdes showed up a little serious, because, despite how she'd always been, this time she didn't want to be the center of attention. On the other hand, she told them:

— "Well, enough! It's not that much! I'm fine and I am happy to see you girls. Now, continue with what you were doing."

Little by little, the euphoria passed for everyone except for Martha Zaida, that still looked at her excited. She patted her back, which was the biggest thing she had done since the moment they met.

Weeks passed and everything went better. Things were aligned and the other women noticed she was different. She laughed more and integrated easily in the conversations. All of them talked behind her back, but it was something they liked.

It was much easier to live with her like that. She also felt different and even her health problems, her diabetes, diminished, except for some intense and sporadic pains. When this happened, she went to the bathroom to wait until they passed, because she didn't want anyone else to notice.

Humberto was very happy with his job as a teacher at college. He felt important and useful, his students appreciated and admired him, and not only for his career but for how he moved on after the accident.

They injected him with a new mood filled with youth and energy. What they didn't know was that his biggest happiness came from his new relationship with his wife. He loved talking with Lourdes about them during the dinner.

There were always anecdotes to tell her and she knew each one of those kids. Because of that teacher, she also learned to love them. Perhaps he was becoming a fatherly old man.

As usual, Lourdes prepared dinner as she waited for Humberto top talk about his day. It was seven in the afternoon and it was getting dark. Humberto still hadn't arrived, which was kind of strange, because when he was delayed, he would always let her know.

She sat at the table in silence and, without knowing exactly why, she felt the phone would ring at any moment. And so it happened: the college contacted her to tell her that Humberto had a stroke and he was taken to a hospital, exactly where their children worked. Lourdes didn't receive more information. Lourdes hung up as if she were a zombie. She took her keys, fetched her bag, and went in the car, without rushing.

While driving, several images crossed her mind, mostly images from the last months that had been wonderful. At heart, she knew that that was over, but she didn't cry, she didn't scream, she did nothing. The silence was overwhelming, her lips couldn't simply be separated, and her face couldn't form any grimace. The reality was so strong that it oppressed her.

She arrived at the hospital. She felt a burden in her body that made her walk slow, her face was very hard, her eyelids were almost closed, and she was ready to hear the worst.

When she got at the entrance, her children came at her with teary eyes. Their faces confirmed the worst. The three of them hugged and that was the moment when Lourdes could vent, screaming in pain, suffering, not understanding what happened. Why now? Why like this?

A devastating stroke during a class, before his students' eyes. It left him without life in an instant, sitting in his wheelchair. Lourdes went to see Humberto's body that lied on a bed. His face looked quiet, like when he slept.

It was the same gesture she saw every morning on him while he was sleeping. In that moment, she felt the urge to move him a little, she couldn't stop thinking that he was probably simply sleeping.

She lied on his chest, missing his heartbeats that during the last months she fell asleep with. She started to cry again, but this time without desperation or pain, only that helpless feeling towards what can't be changed, with resignation.

Her children saw her totally surrendered in that moment. Without words, it seemed as if she thanked him for every instant they had lived together since they had found themselves. That event had been without a doubt the beginning of a new life and no one in that room knew why exactly that life filled with happiness had to end.

Lourdes asked them to leave her alone for a few minutes with Humberto and they left.

— "Humberto my husband... I think your heart stopped because of the amount of love you've given me these months. It worked more than what it was used to and that's why I thank you. I appreciate every instant it beat for me, to show me that I was sick with seriousness, that

I was dried with sadness, because of my selfishness.

It was so easy, Humberto, so easy for us to be happy since we got married. Now I understand that what changed our lives was so easy and we lost it because we didn't want to take the first step, neither of us. Still, I appreciate the time we spent together so much, and I mean these last few months. Our previous years together, I don't count them. I call that co-existence. We were just two people in the same house, sharing the same things, but actually, two people can only be together when their souls recognize each other.

I tell you right now that I'll look for thousands of ways during my next lives to be with you again, until we get to be what everyone is destined to be as a couple. An example of love, understanding, and happiness. I'm sorry for the wasted time. As a tribute to you, I promise you that from now on I'll seize every day as if it was the last one. And when that day comes, I'll meet it happy, knowing you'll be there for me in order to continue walking and get to start again... And, that day, Humberto, will arrive soon."

Lourdes remained on his chest until she was interrupted by the people that left the room. A long time had passed by and she didn't know how much it was, she had even felt she had fallen asleep.

The funeral took place with the proper ceremony. There were crowns, people from the hospital, family, teachers, and students from the college—who looked deeply affected. Humberto had won the hearts of those students pretty fast, which made Lourdes proud. When they walked towards her to offer their condolences, she realized how much they admired Humberto. That filled her with happiness.

She suddenly felt a strong hug, those hugs that filled your soul. It was so sudden that she didn't even know who it was from, she couldn't see the face, she only felt that love in that person's arms.

When she finally got to see who that person was, she was shocked to see Martha Zaida, that woman from the club she considered vulgar. Although the ladies she used to be friends with attended the funeral, no hug felt the same.

She remembered that, one way or another, that woman had always been present, interested in every event of her life; in Humberto's accident, when she was hospitalized, and now in the funeral. Her messages were always read, but never replied, and still she continued, as though she didn't understand, and simply ignored Lourdes' explicit rejection.

Two weeks passed since the burial, and Lourdes was quiet. Her children didn't want to leave her alone. She didn't look good. She had lost weight and was pale.

They thought it was because of the loss they had gone through, but they were worried, although she didn't complain at all.

They went every day in the afternoons and took their spouses and grandchildren with them to cheer Lourdes up, but they realized Lourdes was serene. Lourdes took Humberto's death in a transcendent way. She easily understood, and they also did, in a way, although they didn't stop saying she didn't look good.

The house felt empty. During the day, Lourdes seized the time to take everything that belonged to her husband out of the closet, like clothes, papers, documents, and others. In one of those sessions, she found a sealed folder with her name on it that she never wanted to open. Those were the results the doctor had given her when she was at the hospital and, although it said "urgent," she didn't open it. She knew that intense pain she had felt wasn't something to take lightly, and although at heart she knew what it was, she didn't want to know for sure.

Two weeks after Humberto's death, Lourdes stopped dressing in black, went out in the street and walked towards the park where she and Humberto had met again in that discussion, when they got undressed. She arrived at the park and walked without a rush. She was aware of her breaths, her movements, every instant, and everything that happened around her. She felt more alive than ever.

She found a bench where the sunbeams seemed to sit and, after sitting in there, she sunk in her conscious thoughts that no one would ever know. She decided she would make those days the most important ones of her life. She'd try some things she never tried before; she thought of the things she would have liked doing. While walking on the streets, she threw the folder with the results in a trashcan without opening it.

After two blocks, she found herself before a theater, a place she'd never visited, even though it was at the same block. She looked at the banner and was impressed by the title of the play: "Undressed relationships."

She always had prejudices about things before she got to know them and surely, years ago, she would have never thought of attending something called that way. She would have looked immoral, she would have been shocked, thinking of the kind of sick man that would name a play like that, without even knowing what it was that about.

Nevertheless, that day, she would do everything she would have never done. She realized she was on time for the show, so she bought a ticket and got in to see the play. Perhaps it was a matter of luck, but there was just one seat at the center.

That afternoon, she decided to live every minute during the play intensely. She felt free, enjoying whatever came. She laughed and cried like she had never done before, like she would have loved to do. She simply lived.

When leaving that room, she thought of that woman she used to judge because of her laughing, the woman that seemed so common and irresponsible, that also had two divorces and a child from each marriage. Yes, Martha Zaida.

That play had such a meaning... Something changed in her, because she immediately felt guilty for having been so harsh towards Martha Zaida. She decided to call her to tell her to go to the theater to see the play she just saw, but the woman didn't pick up, so she left a message.

— "Hi, Martha Zaida. How are you? I've called you, but you're surely busy. I know, this may seem strange for you, as I never did it before. We never spoke too much, only when we met at the cafe or the club, but I'll tell you what I am calling you for. I've always criticized you. For me you always looked like a low-value woman. I want you to know that you were never that. I now realize that I envied that freedom of yours you always acted with, because I didn't have it. I just left the theater and I want you to come and see this play called "Undressed Relationships." This isn't a suggestion, and way less an invitation. It's a special request for you.

You don't know this, but I'm dying. As you'd imagine, I have no time to lie.
I want to apologize to you for having been so harsh and cruel. Although I never told you the things I thought of you, I know you noticed my indifference and my arrogance. You'll always be in my memories as a brave woman that always knew how to be happy, no matter what happened. Now I know that it wasn't irresponsibility. It was flexibility before a change, it was resilience. I hug you at a distance..."

After leaving that voice message, she walked to her home, satisfied she did that and with a big smile on her lips. She didn't care that the sky was dark, that the streets were dark, that it was cold. She simply stopped thinking of "what could have happened" and focused on every instant she was living.

Every step seemed to her like an artwork. How many things had to happen so she could execute just one movement! While reflecting about this, she breathed the fresh air that filled her lungs deeply and slowly. She heard the leaves' sound floating with the wind, she enjoyed the cold on her face, she even closed her eyes for a moment, so every sensation could become more intense.

Lourdes was totally and absolutely present in every moment of her life. She realized that, finally, she was living at her best and didn't wish this to end, but she knew that would happen too.

She felt a certain wish to cry she couldn't contain. Her tears left her eyes so wonderfully that she enjoyed that too. She'd never been conscious of the incredible miracle that was to transform a feeling into a liquid leaving her eyes.

God! What an intense sensation of gratitude for the incredible artwork that her body was! She was discovering things she always lived with, but she never knew, exactly like how it had happened with Humberto.

She arrived home and as she opened the door, she heard the phone ringing. She couldn't answer it and she didn't do much for it. She was so fulfilled she didn't want anything to distract her from her **CONSCIOUS BEING** *that she just found, because she felt she was falling in love with that sensation and she just wanted to enjoy it.*

She went to her room calmly. She continued happy of having found that play. It was the first time she did it and she knew it wasn't by chance that she saw that play that night. It was such a clear sign that made her feel so fulfilled, although she barely enjoyed walking from the theater to home.

The phone sounded again and this time she answered. It was her son Aldo. He was worried. They went home to see her, but they didn't find her. They waited for a while thinking she was just going to be out for a few minutes, but time went by and she didn't arrive. They were very worried for her, after so many complicated events.

Lourdes asked her son to calm down and to let his brother know she was at home already. She told him that she went out to walk and went to a play. Her son was happy to know she was well, but he was surprised by that news. It was good to know his mother was living things she hadn't lived. They hung up, not without saying "I love you."

She walked towards her closet, where she kept her pajamas, the same Humberto had gently pulled out of the closet the day she returned from the hospital, to give to her. That was the perfect excuse to be close to her, that was his love's excuse.

She cried again and then she felt that pain come, the one that made her go to the closest bathroom to get on the floor and roll around without anyone noticing. But the pain was now more intense.

She couldn't move, she could barely get to the bed and scream in the silence. No one was there physically, but she knew the moment was close and someone was waiting for her in another place.

That hope reduced the killing pain that seemed eternal. Little by little she calmed down until she was allowed to open the drawer to look for a sheet of paper and a pen, but not enough to call her children.

As it was expected, the news was rapidly known. The very next day, her friends from the exercise group arrived at the funeral, among them, of course, Martha Zaida.

Everything had been so hectic that she hadn't noticed the message Lourdes had left her the previous afternoon. It was just after the funeral that she heard it, and of course, it was shocking for her.

Those words totally tore her apart. It was a fight of feelings in which no one knew which was the strongest one; if it was the pain of the death of that woman she admired so much, the one she had never been a close friend to but always wished to be, or discovering the image Lourdes had about her...

She was confused, but there was no doubt she was suffering.

The next day, in the morning, she bought the newspaper to look for the play Lourdes wanted her to see. It was necessary, she was very curious, and wished to know what it was all about. In the newspaper, she saw that that was the last day of the show, and she ran to the theater to get a ticket.

She got dressed as though she was going to see the play of her life. She combed her hair and did her makeup. She did a good job, she didn't want anyone to notice she had been crying. She was waiting to see what sort of mystery Lourdes Vargas' intensions hid.

Sitting at the center of the room, Martha Zaida observed carefully:

> "Now, before dying, I'd like to know what I have learned and if someone listened to me carefully, they'd understand my words are just a reflection of what I've lived.
>
> I spent a lot of time trying to understand that the present isn't today, it's not here and now. The present is being like this, **in presence**, present, realizing what happens. And now, exactly when I'm told I have a few days to live, I find that my existence's essence was to always be thinking, meditating, reflecting, analyzing, with my head in the past, with a future promise;

I was finally going to find good things, but, the only thing I found was feeling guilt, sorrow, and pain.

My mind took me there and then threw me to a future, anticipating what was coming, although it did it to make me worried and anxious. This anxiety made me try to be a good woman and I now find that, between my past and future goals, I forgot to be present.

These last years I've felt what it's like to be present in the present. Not like a today, here, now, but like an instant, conscious of what happens in this thing that moves and that I know as 'me.'

I've discovered my feelings, I know my source of energy is in my relationships, and all of my relationships were based on a 'should be' created by my heard, because of my wish to reach a level of happiness and fulfillment that never arrived. Now I've found that life and energy show up when I am able to experience what I am given in the moment."

She was the last one to leave the theater. She stood as if she was in a movie where everyone passed by her quickly while she moved slowly. She walked among the seats, crossed the reception, and as she left the theater, her eyes were filled with tears that she couldn't contain. She didn't feel sad nor lonely, she felt a series of emotions that she didn't recognize, but they were associated with satisfaction.

She immediately felt she needed to talk to Lourdes and tell her everything, although she knew she wasn't there anymore. She was anxious like a little kid. Besides, nothing would have changed, because all those years, Lourdes never answered one of her calls.

It started raining, softly, but with wind. She looked at the sky and closed her eyes with her cellphone at hand. For the first time, she enjoyed the rain as if it was something new, something different, something that she wouldn't have seen before and, with that freedom, she left a brief message when she heard the tone, feeling an enormous wave of gratitude that drowned her with every word.

— "Lourdes, what's up? I'd like to tell you plenty of stuff, but I realized that I took so much to understand that the present isn't today, that it's not here and now. The present is being like this, in presence... Present."

She continued talking, every time with more and more speed and less pauses, about her anxiety and being happy, about her permanent career and achieving success, a corrupted success that was filled with promises that made her mind live in a permanent state of dissatisfaction, filled with ghosts from the past and postponed ideas for the future.

And, suddenly, just now, just there, in the middle of the street, under that tender rain, she had found herself able to experience the present. The moment, that brief instant.

She couldn't stop talking until the recorder interrupted her. Then she ran to the sidewalk in front of her. As if called from destiny, the store where she could protect herself from rain was a small library filled with colors and elements that reminded her of her youth.

She got excited when she realized she was in there and she seized the apparent coincidence to buy some paper, pencils, pens, envelopes, and even stickers.

She felt as though she was in a party! When the rain stopped, she ran home without losing her change. She didn't stop getting surprised and continued smiling.

After she arrived, she took a hot bath. She had the urge to clear her mind. She put on her favorite pajamas.

She took her time to make hot chocolate and toasted bread and finally, at the dining table, she put before her the piece of paper and pencils.

She looked at the piece of paper for a while and without fear she took the pencil and started writing:

> "Now, just before I die, I'd like to
> say everything I've learned..."

She tore the piece of paper and started again, over and over again, until her head, soul, and hand were synchronized.

"Dear everyone,

I wish to be sincere with all of you and I trust you can read me, although I won't be here to see your faces and hug all of you. If you read me with attention, you'll understand my words are not only the reflection of what I've lived, but the surprise from my late discovery.

For years, I lived under my beliefs. I spent so much time trying to understand that the present isn't today, isn't the here and now. The present is remaining like this, in presence, present. I admit I've had my moments filled with doubts and questions, but at heart, in my soul, I discovered through my faith that my life's essence isn't thinking or analyzing the past or the future. I've discovered that life and energy exist when I am capable of experiencing what I am going through during that moment.

I know, it's been difficult. My lack of positivity, my negative mindset, my complaints, my cries, my silence, my stress, and all those things—it's not necessary to say that I haven't had the best year, that I haven't been the best sister, friend, and person, but despite everything, I appreciate your love, tenderness, and patience with me. I hope you can understand me and learn from this woman that discovered there's no need to make a huge effort to be fulfilled, too late."

God: **wherever** you are and **whoever** you are,
I'm ready to receive you with arms wide
open and my heart filled with love!

Contenido

www.ingramcontent.com/pod-product-compliance
Lightning Source LLC
Chambersburg PA
CBHW032046090426
42744CB00004B/104